When Your
Business
Partner
is Your Spouse

Cheers to Happiness AND Success!

Justin & Kristen Deese

When Your
Business
Partner
is Your Spouse

HOW TO HAVE A Successful Business
AND A Happy Marriage

Kristen & Justin Deese

gatekeeper press

Columbus, Ohio

When Your Business Partner is Your Spouse: How to
Have a Successful Business AND a Happy Marriage

Published by Gatekeeper Press
2167 Stringtown Rd, Suite 109
Columbus, OH 43123-2989
www.GatekeeperPress.com

ISBN (hardcover): 9781642379747
ISBN (paperback): 9781642379754
eISBN: 9781642379761

CONTENTS

Dedication 7

Acknowledgements 9

Disclaimer 11

Chapter 1   Introduction...13

Chapter 2   The Vision..22

Chapter 3   Take the Clock by the Hands.......................47

Chapter 4   Setting and Sticking to Clearly
Defined Roles 67

Chapter 5   Communication 80

Chapter 6   Your Social Circle.. 101

Chapter 7   Boundaries 116

Chapter 8   Strong Body, Strong Mind 132

Chapter 9   Reaping the Benefits 147

Epilogue   161

DEDICATION

To the successful business owners we look up to as mentors,
&
all those that choose to be married
AND own a business together.

ACKNOWLEDGEMENTS

This book has been nearly 20 years in the making, and it could not have been done without some pretty incredible people who have come into our lives. I am a firm believer in coaching of any sort. I believe that those who have a strong foundation in their unique abilities and who also desire to help others realize their true potential are the most profound and effective coaches there are. Our writing coach, Sara Connell, was instrumental in the creation of this literary masterpiece. ☺ Sara, without your knowledge, system, support and accountability we never would have been able to make this happen. You are unbelievably incredible and talented, and your energy and drive are contagious. Thank you for sharing all of that with us!

We have learned firsthand that coaching is instrumental in making stuff happen, and that could not be truer of our experience with our business coach, Christina Ellis. Christina, you changed our lives. You pushed us, held us accountable, taught us countless invaluable lessons and above all believed in us. You changed our trajectory and will forever hold a special place in our hearts. We are so grateful that you were placed in our lives at exactly the right time!

It goes without saying—but I am going to say it anyway—the content for this book would not have been available without my entrepreneurial husband. Justin, I heard you say on a podcast recently that a bored entrepreneur is dangerous—that could not be truer! Even though this life we have made is so much different than so many others, we wouldn't be where we are today without your drive and motivation to keep pushing forward and be the best we can be for me and the kids. We love you all the time!

And lastly, I am so humbled to have worked with our coaching clients, the fellow business owners that have crossed our path during their various stages of business development. Our goal with you all is to provide a different perspective and hold a space for you to step into your full potential as successful entrepreneurs. Your businesses are invaluable to our economic society and without your deep and profound desire to own a successful business, our options to consume would be monopolized.

DISCLAIMER

Without the stories involving those around us, this book would be pretty boring. We have changed the details of the stories and examples that aren't about Justin and me to protect the anonymity of our family, friends and fellow business owners. Our goal weaved among these words and pages is for you, the reader, to take away at least one nugget you can apply to your life and to realize that there are people out there that are in or have been in the same boat. Others have struggled through your business challenges and celebrated your business celebrations, just like you. You are not alone, and there is help out there if you want it.

CHAPTER 1

Introduction

*"I think it is possible for ordinary people to
choose to be extraordinary."* —Elon Musk

From the outside looking in, our life was picture perfect. Justin and I were in our late twenties. We had a beautiful, brand new home in the suburbs of Atlanta. We drove nice cars, had nice things, and threw large parties. We had two young children, one dog and one cat. The house was always clean, and laundry always done. We were social with our neighbors, attended church on Sunday, and said, "Cheese," before every picture.

Sound great?

Well, under that façade was another picture. As married business partners, we were also stressed to the max and at the edge of destruction. Our finances were out of control, and we were so unbearably busy all the time that it was easier to keep digging the hole than it was to figure out how to get out of it. So, we hid it. We hid it from friends and family. We hid it from our employees and clients. We even tried to hide it from ourselves.

The beginning of business ownership was exciting and motivating. Every small victory was a big win for us. Every check made out to our incorporation name was a victory in our books. It didn't take long for the toll of business ownership to bare its ugly head though. We sailed right through the honeymoon stage of running a business and straight into the trenches of war between us and the world.

Perhaps you know the depths of the trenches we refer to? The pressure of making sure customers are satisfied and money is in the bank to cover payroll for the employees who rely on you, so they can feed their families. Vendors you are purchasing from and personal credit you are using to operate day to day operations are constantly knocking at your door. How about the employees? They need to be led, trained and managed. Wow, that takes a whole lot more time than you initially thought it would, right?

It's one thing to own a business, and a whole other challenge to do so with a spouse. Not only are you trying to keep a business afloat, with multiple employees relying on your ability to do so, but you also have a spouse and kids relying on you to do so as well. Plus, your spouse is your business partner which has the potential of adding another layer of pressure to an already stressful situation.

Justin and I never set out to be entrepreneurs, but we were certainly not average either. We met as teenagers; he was 19

and I was 17. We advanced from entry level retail jobs to middle management at a far younger age than our peers. We are intelligent, risk averse people. As very young adults, we bought a house and cars. We were always current with the trending technological devices. We had friends in the neighborhood, one of whom worked for an alcohol distribution company and filled his garage to the brim with every kind of libation you could imagine. We went house hopping and bar hopping on weekends, attended concerts and enjoyed what life had to offer for those that could easily function on only a few hours of sleep at night. We lived to have fun, work hard and succeed, at someone else's established company.

Justin has always been the dreamer. The visionary. The go-getter. The hustler. When we found ourselves in a bind, he was going to be the half of us that found a solution and usually said solution was anything but ordinary. I suppose if you had to label him with only one word, you would say he's the entrepreneur.

I am exactly opposite in just about every way. I like order and consistency. I always have a plan and can get pretty bent out of shape when the plan changes at the last minute. I like security and predictability. And I am one hundred percent introverted with a dry sense of humor. I recently took a personality test and my introverted rating was 99—the highest possible score was 100. Looks like an A+ to me!

Our opposition on personality traits is a large part of what makes us work so well together. We have worked together in some form for basically all of our relationship. For the first several years we both worked at "normal" jobs getting some foundation in the business world, learning the basics of what it meant to be an employee.

I was working at a salon, and Justin was working as a recruiter for fiber optics technicians. He had a pretty good gig. It included sales and commission which was right up his alley. We were living in Georgia in a little newly constructed house we bought as a pile of dirt at the age of 19. It was a new neighborhood at the time with hundreds of houses that all looked the same, each one set fourteen feet from the house on either side. A great little starter home. We had made several good friends on our street. Our next-door neighbors were our age and in the same chapter of our lives. Both of them worked full-time, Monday through Friday 9 am to 5 pm jobs. They didn't have any kids yet, but they were wonderful dog parents.

I distinctly remember the day that changed our trajectory. Kelly, our neighbor, had a little concrete bench in the flower bed in front of her house. I came home from the salon one afternoon when Justin normally would have been at the office to find him sitting on Kelly's concrete bench. I thought, "What in the world is he doing?" I got out of the truck and was like, "Hey, what in the world are you doing over there?"

I don't even remember what he said but when he spoke, I immediately knew he was drunk. Now remember, we were in our early 20s, so day drinking wasn't all that uncommon, but it was not like him to skip out on work to do so. I knew something was up. Kelly came out when I got home and told me she found him there when she arrived too, and he had obviously had a bad day. She left him on her bench and went on about her afternoon.

Justin and I went inside, sat down at the kitchen table and he told me that he had been laid off. I am sure there was a variety of reasons why he was laid off, and I am also sure that work ethic or personality conflicts were not the reasons he was cut. I'm not just saying that because I have a biased opinion. I could see the defeat on his face and hear it in his voice as he told me about the events of the day. Then he said, "We bought this house, and now we are going to lose it because I don't have a job. I don't have a college education. I have no specific trade training. Who is going to hire me?"

The fear in his eyes penetrated my soul. Justin was freaking out and for the first time in his life, he attributed the vulnerable state we found ourselves in because of a decision made by another human in a business that he had no control over.

Initially, I was shocked at the news of Justin getting laid off, but I can't say I was ever in fear. I knew deep down that Justin had enough drive to find another job, so I wasn't worried about that. It did hurt me to see him hurting though, and I did my best to stay strong during his moment of perceived weakness. Here we were, sitting in a new house with a $1300 a month mortgage payment, which in the year 2000 for people our age was a lot of money, and his income which accounted for 60% of our joint finances was now gone. I remember telling him it was ok; everything would be fine. He could go down to the unemployment office in the morning and get that paperwork going. We would update his resume, and he could hit the streets the next day to find another job. Any employer would be lucky to have him on their team.

Then it happened. I didn't know what changed, but his face unwrinkled itself. Something like a beam of sun passed over his eyes. I didn't know what because he had not voiced the thought aloud, but IT happened. The thought that shaped the rest of our lives...

Screw them! Never again will one person be able to negatively influence my future or the future of my family. Never will I be bound by the ties of being an employee at another's company. The thought that comes to every entrepreneur. The thought that seduces each one of us onto the wild, unpredictable sea. The unemployment office was slipping away like a shoreline. Justin no longer wanted to be the employee, he wanted to be the *employer*.

Ok, I thought. Let's not get ahead of ourselves. The calm sense that comes from a good plan, like find another job, faded fast from my mind and I started to get nervous. Going a couple weeks without a paycheck from him might suck, but starting a business contains way more uncertainty than job hunting, and uncertainty immediately breeds fear in me.

What was this business going to be? We had no money saved, half the regular income no longer coming in, and he wanted to take the risk of starting a business? What if it were too much like the business you were just laid off from and they sue you for violating a non-compete? What if no money comes in from it? What if it fails? If it does, will you go get a *real* job?? These were the panicked thoughts in my mind the first day he set out to become an entrepreneur.

That day he was up at dawn, dressed, showered and out the door.

"Don't worry," Justin said. "I don't have a plan, but I'll figure it out."

Shortly after that day, his first official business was born. He started a recruiting company in the field of telecommunications. Basically, he would be a contracted head-hunter. I was skeptical of the entire idea, but he was pretty fired up. I kept my job and figured I'd give it a few weeks, all the while secretly hoping the idea of entrepreneurism would soon fizzle out, and he'd just go get a job like the rest of people our age.

Not long after he started that business, he received his first payment for services rendered. The check that arrived in the mail was $32,000. That was more than he would have brought home in a whole year written right there on one check in our barely adult hands!

That was a motivating event and further solidified Justin's desire to never again work for anyone else. That was it, I thought, so much for him getting a *real* job.

That business was a turning point for Justin. For him, it represented the transition from a guy trying to start a business to a guy who owned a business. It served as his adrenaline rush, his motivation to keep striving for more. And that's exactly what he did. He always reached for more. Always wanted bigger and better, but owning and running various businesses took a toll on our lives.

Within a few short years we started to feel the real effects of entrepreneurialism. We suffered through many of the unfortunately common pitfalls that many business owners succumb to like not having any time outside of the business, unpredictable cash flow, communication issues and operating in a constant state of overwhelm.

One of the things we never anticipated losing was the connection with our social circle, but we eventually learned that not only did we not have time to hang out with our friends but when we did, there were fewer and fewer things we could find to talk about. Our lives were taking a turn that theirs wasn't, and the things we all had in common before dried and shriveled like a plant with no water.

We felt broken down, isolated and shackled to our business. There were countless times that we were ready to throw in the towel. Call it good. Close up shop. Get a *real* job. At this point, neither of us wanted to go back to work for other people; we may not even be qualified to do so anymore. But we couldn't keep going the way we were in which our finances, marriage, and children's wellbeing were all being compromised. We were on a fast descent into physical, financial and emotional collapse.

But, we found reserves of strength, determination fueled with desperation. We dug our way out of that abyss. How? In the exact ways we're going to show you in this book.

Today we're in a great place. Our marriage, businesses and children are thriving. We have financial freedom, and all the exciting experiences that go with it but most importantly we are personally and individually fulfilled and are living our purpose every single day. That personal fulfillment allows us to give whole-heartedly to our marriage, our children and our businesses and that, my friends, is an incredible place to be.

We didn't have a road map or a guide. We stumbled upon some of what saved us by reaching out for support, getting help and some by dumb luck. What we want to share with you in this book is that there IS a way to co-own a successful business as a married couple and thrive in all areas of business and life. We invite you to come along as we dig deep on our journey as married business partners. We are pulling back the curtain to reveal a more vulnerable side of our powerhouse, and there will be times when we will ask you to become vulnerable, too. Those places can be scary, but it is from those shadows where true growth emerges. It won't always be easy, but we can tell you beyond a shadow of a doubt and with 100% certainty that it will be well worth it!

Here's a little fable for your enjoyment:

> *A guy is walking down the street when he falls in a hole. The walls are so steep he can't get out. A doctor passes by and the guy shouts up, "Hey you, can you help me out?"*

The doctor writes him a prescription, throws it down in the hole and moves on.

Then a priest comes along and the guy shouts up, "Father, I'm down in this hole, can you help me out?"

The priest writes out a prayer, throws it down in the hole and moves on.

Then a friend walks by. "Hey Joe, it's me, can you help me out?"

The friend jumps in the hole. The guy says, "Are you stupid? Now we're both down here!"

The friend says, "Yeah, but I've been down here before and I know the way out."

CHAPTER 2

The Vision

*"If you don't know where you are going any
road will get you there."* —Cheshire Cat

There was a point in time where Justin said, "Yes," to everything. Every shiny object. Never would he turn down an opportunity to receive money. It didn't matter if the opportunity had nothing to do with our current business trajectory, any opportunity that presented itself was an opportunity and he was going to take it. It was irrelevant if he had never done what was being presented to him. A manager, a contractor, a neighbor would ask him to do a job, and Justin would smile, nod confidently and tell the person not to worry that we could do it. The yes-man in him had us jumping from one thing to another. Early on, it was fish tank maintenance, then it was employee recruiting, and later on it was a pizzeria. At one point we even had a basement full of ground coffee bags that he was negotiating shelf space for at local grocery and convenience stores. Justin said, "Yes," to these projects, and then he would run home, and we'd spend the next hours, days, even weeks completely submersing ourselves trying to figure out how in the world we were going to handle the new challenge laid before us.

Saying, "Yes," to every opportunity, as a matter of fact, is the philosophy of a handful of some successful and wealthy businesspeople. "Never say, 'No,' to money" is the popular mantra of a national entrepreneur group. However, saying, "Yes," to every opportunity can also deplete your resources, leave you personally and professionally drained, and in some cases even cause catastrophic consequences.

Saying, "Yes," to every opportunity can grow your business. But saying, "No," can propel you from successful to *very* successful. But we didn't know that yet.

Saying, "No," is as unthinkable to most entrepreneurs as lighting a stack of hundred-dollar bills on fire. For Justin and me, the thought of saying, "No," never so much as crossed our minds. Ever.

As committed as we were to our *yes* philosophy, the negative effects of always saying, "Yes," to everything ran through our business like the plague. The main reason this was the case was that we had no vision or plan for the future. At first there was a vision: it was called "generating cash." The initial and informal vision was painfully short-sighted. This vision never considered how that money generated would be spent or for what services the money would be paid and from whom.

One decision after another, month after month, year after year, in what felt like an instant, we found ourselves running a giant business that, from the outside, appeared to be very successful. We were installing kitchen appliances for big box retailers in five states. There were about 35 trucks on the road generating $5M in sales a year. We were creating a name for ourselves in the industry. Except we weren't running the business, the rest of the world was. Our customers, vendors and even employees were running all over us because we had no vision or goals for the company. We spent every single day just trying to keep our head above water. Yes, our world without vision was dismal. Never could we lay our heads down at night and feel like the day was a win. Within the depths of overwhelm, every day started with waking up to the undeniable feeling of dread deep in the stomach. A feeling of being behind before the day ever got started. Running on a treadmill to nowhere. We weren't making headway, and that was so incredibly unmotivating.

This is why saying, "Yes," to everything was so tempting and easy. We were at a point in our business that we needed cash flow to support the expenses, so if the opportunity came up that looked like incoming cash, then we accepted regardless of how much it cost to generate that cash and whether or not it related to our current business trajectory. In our minds, increased sales equated to growth, and growth equated to success and if we were generating $5M a year in sales, then we had to be successful. But was this what successful was supposed to feel like? Was this some horrible secret that the successful hid from the rest of the world—that success was equivalent to misery? Certainly, that's not the case…right?

KRISTEN

Payroll was a huge area of resentment for many years. We were moving money from one bank account to another crossing our fingers the next deposit would hit the bank at least 60 seconds before the payroll withdrawal would hit. If the deposit didn't show up, and there weren't enough funds in the account to cover payroll, then it would get kicked back. So many times I had wished that our bank would let the payroll ACH overdraw our account, but it wasn't that way. In order for payroll to clear, the money had to be there, no exceptions. Our payroll withdrawals at that time were around $50k each, and it always seemed like when we were short, we were *really* short.

The weight of managing the cash flow fell heavy on my shoulders. I was the financial professional between the two of us, so it was obvious from the onset that's one of the things I would do. I remember one time when the pressure of that was so unbelievably intense. It was a payroll week, and I was going through the typical steps of moving money around in preparation for the gigantic withdrawal that was scheduled to hit that night at midnight. This time was different though. This time there wasn't enough money. We were short, and not by a little bit.

I was standing in the driveway working on my laptop that was propped on our open truck tailgate and tilted, so I could see the screen despite the mid-afternoon sun. Our 2-year-old son was pushing his dump trucks around in the grass on his knees and making the sound effects of a huge earth moving project only he could see in his imagination. As I moved from one online account to the next, making transfers into the account where payroll would soon be withdrawn, it became clear that we had a huge problem. The close of the business banking day was nearing, and after moving all available cash into the account from which the payroll would be taken and adding in the anticipated deposit coming that night, I realized this time we wouldn't make it. We'd been here before, but the transfer had always scraped through in time. This time, the gap was too far. And there wasn't anything I could do about it.

A wave of anxiety overcame me as I dropped to the ground. I couldn't feel my hands and feet, couldn't catch my breath, and the color was gone from my cheeks despite the intense heat I felt from within. There were three thoughts that circled in my head like vultures flying over roadkill. How was I going to get everyone paid? What was I going to tell the employees? I had to tell Justin. That last thought was the worst. I had placed so much pressure on myself over the years of juggling these ugly cashflow balls that when I dropped one, I felt like I was a complete failure. I was one of the two legs that supported this business and when I failed, Justin had to carry the extra weight. I knew he was going to be extremely angry, partly at me but mostly that we worked so damn hard and still struggled with covering payroll. The last thing I wanted was to be the one to have to tell him we weren't going to make payroll for fear that one of these days a bucket of bad news was going to be the shove that puts him over the edge.

I called him up and delivered the news and held my breath bracing for his initial reaction. The conversation mirrored what I had imagined. He was angry, of course—not really at me but at the entire thing. I just happened to be the messenger on the other end of the line that got to hear the unedited version of feelings evoked by this particular issue. After that initial 30 seconds of shock, anger and depression—who knew you could feel and express such extreme feelings in such a short period of time—we both turned to the what-do-we-do-next plan.

Well, the first thing we did was stop our checks. There was no way Justin and I were going to try to take a check that week and if someone was going to get paid late, we would be the first ones on the list, no question. Then we reached out to our area managers and let them know that the direct deposit wouldn't be going through, so we were going to have live checks cut for everyone that week. Justin and I figured that only about half of the employees would run out to the bank and deposit the checks on Friday and the rest, for various reasons, would wait until Monday. By Monday the account would have enough to cover the rest of the checks, so we were relying on the procrastinators in the company to cover up the fact that they were getting paid late. We told everyone that we had made a mistake submitting the direct deposit; we didn't dare tell them the mistake was in the lack of cash. After all, if the employees caught wind that we might be in some sort of cash crisis, they might jump ship and then, what would we do?

We made it through that payroll challenge, but it was messy. Bad enough to light an ember of desire in me. The desire to find a better way. I knew there would be another payroll crisis soon. We might have a month's reprieve, but it would happen again. At night I lay awake thinking, hoping that there was some better way to make this business work while keeping our sanity and our marriage intact. There had to be. And we had to find it…soon.

Looking back on this moment, not having enough cash for payroll was merely a symptom of a much larger problem. This was a problem that we couldn't see from our vantage point at that time because we were so deeply engulfed in this directionally challenged monster of a business we had created. We were lost amongst the trees of our very own national forest.

It took quite a while after that payroll crisis to get to our turning point. We spent months simply trying to figure out what *help* looked like. The conversation of closing the doors on the entire business came up often. On one hand it sounded like such an easy way to be freed from this nightmare, but on the other hand, we were generating millions of dollars a year in sales—that had to be worth something and we didn't want to walk away leaving cash on the table. There it is again. Cash. It was too painful to say, "No," to the opportunity for incoming cash which was one reason closing the doors looked a lot less appealing than selling.

One day Justin presented me with an idea he had been researching. "We need a business coach," he proclaimed.

A business coach? I didn't even know what that meant. What was a business coach, and how could they help? I didn't care, any help they could provide I'd be willing to accept. So, we scheduled our first call.

The day came for our first call with our business coach. Justin was in the field that day and wouldn't be available to talk, so it was my responsibility to represent the both of us. Even during this first call we were not committed to coaching, nor was she committed to coaching us. It was almost like we were interviewing each other to see if a coaching relationship would be worthwhile to both the coach and the client. I entered that call feeling anxious, overwhelmed and slightly ticked that Justin couldn't carve out an hour to do this with me. Remember, it was his idea to begin with and now on the very first call, he wasn't participating.

The call with Christina, the business coach we were paired with, went well despite the fact that Justin wasn't there. She was able to connect with me and my pain points, and a few tears rolled down my cheeks at one point during our call. Until then, I only cried in front of Justin. At that point in my life, crying felt like weakness and vulnerability, and I did everything I could to not let anyone see that side of me. Christina did a great job making me feel safe to express exactly what I thought, felt and struggled with about the business without judgement. I couldn't do that with anyone else besides Justin, and it was refreshing to talk with an unbiased, unjaded person about where we were in our professional journey.

We wrapped up that first call with me wanting to start coaching right away, but I knew it was expensive, and we were already in a constant cash crunch. I also knew we needed this more than we had ever needed anything before. This was something we had to say, "Yes," to. Now I just needed to get Justin on board with that monthly coaching expense.

A couple weeks later we were on the phone again with Christina for our first official coaching call. My expectations were that she had a system we could follow to get the business on track, and I was just going to do whatever she said we needed to do. Justin, however, had some other expectations of what coaching was. He was expecting a quick fix and wanted to start solving current frustrations right away.

The first thing we did in coaching was create our vision for the company but before we could do that, we had to imagine what our perfect day would look like. I will admit, trying to daydream about what my ideal day would look like was more difficult than it sounds. It's hard to dream about what you want to be doing when what you are currently doing takes up all available brain space. We even wrote our own eulogy which helped change our mindset, so we could think bigger. The eulogy exercise was one profound and effective way to put inconsequential worries into perspective.

Justin was chomping at the bit for our coach to tell us how to fix our company right now. He didn't see how writing his eulogy had anything to do with solving our problems and was resistant to move forward in the process. He was looking for a quick fix, someone to come in, wave a magic wand and poof, a beautiful, successful, fulfilling business appears out of thin air.

That's not at all what happened. There were several times throughout coaching that Justin would get antsy and want to stop, i.e., to save the money, if he didn't see immediate results from what we were working on. Each time I'd do my best to calm his anxiousness and encourage him to trust the process. Today, we are both eternally grateful that we stayed with our coach even when we couldn't see the forest through the trees. She held a place for us to learn and grow professionally and personally which was exactly what we needed despite the fact that we didn't even know what we needed.

No matter where you are in your business, whether you are in the exuberant early stages or you have been worn down and completely depleted, these vision exercises lay a crucial foundation for positive change to point you in the right direction.

At first, just like in our business life, we were overwhelmed by the concept of creating our vision. We edited countless versions; each time our coach would coax out a little more, stretch us to reach even deeper into the purpose and goals we wanted for our business. Once we stopped resisting and surrendered to the process, we worked for several weeks creating our vision using the same exercises we are going to share with you in this chapter.

A business vision statement is not a business plan, but it can be included within the business plan should you choose to create a business plan. A vision describes what the business will look like in 3-5 years, and it goes into details including location, size, sales, net profits, customer description, company culture and competitive advantage. The vision can be described as a photograph of your future business which gives your business shape and direction. When business owners take time to really think about the direction they want for their businesses, decision-making is infinitely easier and more efficient. If the opportunity points towards your vision, then there's a good chance saying, "Yes," would be a good thing. If it points in a direction that's different from your vision, then it makes it easy to say, "Thank you, but no thank you."

Creating a vision is the time to dream big. Uncovering what you really want your business to look like. This work can be exhilarating but the task can also be difficult, especially if you are coming from a state of overwhelm.

We were so locked down by the negative mindset of our business when we began this process that our coach had to break the vision work down step by step, into exercises we could access and do, each one empowering us to go further. The first exercise our business coach presented us with was writing our eulogy. That's right, we were invited to write our own eulogy... what we hoped people would say about us at our funeral after we had lived a long and fruitful life. Even though the idea was presented to both of us as a team, we were encouraged to spend time working on this assignment by ourselves first.

KRISTEN

Being asked to write my own eulogy was a humbling and emotional experience. Death is one of those topics most of us try to avoid. We don't want to think about what might happen if we, our spouse or other loved one died. Expressing what I want people to say about me after I passed forced me to think about desires that up until then remained unspoken. They were unspoken because verbalizing what I wanted people to say about me outside of the context of this exercise had the potential of coming off as arrogant and self-centered. But within the boundaries of this exercise we were able to explore the meaning of our lives—perhaps not the current meaning but the meaning at the end, when life was all said and done. I was asked to go deep and decide what I wanted my life to represent when I was no longer here, after I'd had an entire lifetime to make an impact, make a difference, even if it was just for a small handful of the six billion people on this planet.

The thought process and mindset required to write your own eulogy gives you the opportunity to disassociate from yourself. It allows you to look at your life through the lens of a third party. Many times, the act of disassociating yourself from your situation can be like observing the ground from a hot air balloon. Something that seems like a major problem from ground level becomes remarkably smaller and more manageable from the basket of the balloon floating high in the air. Writing your eulogy encourages you to step into the basket and view your entire life from an aerial perspective. New ideas may emerge. Issues that feel like heavy burdens may fall away like the sandbags cut from the sides of the hot air balloon.

JUSTIN

When I wrote my eulogy, it became clear to me quickly that the most important part of life and what I valued most was time spent with my family. It wasn't time spent in the business or with employees or customers. Ironically, I realized, the business that I had created to support my wife and kids was what was keeping me from all of them. The business that I intended to be a means of independence for us had turned into a shackle. It kept me from experiencing the life I wanted to experience, it kept us from our kids, and it kept us from each other.

I think business owners often get so intertwined with their business that it becomes a part of them, a part of their identity. We fear if we lose the business, we will lose our purpose, our identity. So, we cling to that business with everything we have while our loved ones wait in line for any scraps of attention left over after we've fed the insatiable appetite of the out of control business.

This was one of the more difficult exercises for me to complete. It required me to uncover thoughts and emotions that until then I would have rather left covered up. For that reason, it's important for me to share my eulogy with you, in hopes it will help you get the most from such a vulnerable exercise.

JUSTIN'S EULOGY

Here lies a wonderful husband and father, a man that worked hard and played harder. Justin was someone who was never afraid to go against the grain to achieve his objective. His favorite poem was "The Road Not Taken" by Robert Frost, and I believe it described his life and how happy he was about the chances he took and the path he chose in his life. He was a well-respected leader in the community and someone who lived not a good life but a GREAT LIFE.

I would use the following adjectives to describe him:

Loyal, Honest, Open Minded, Great Listener, Passionate, Giving, Optimistic, Humorous and most of all Fun-Loving

Justin lived a very fortunate life and with his vast amount of wealth, he was able to help many people. He was also able to see the world with his family and was able to be married to the most wonderful woman in the world for the past 74 years.

In his 98 years on this planet, Justin Deese has definitely left this earth a better place than he found it.

KRISTEN

When we'd written our eulogies, our coach had us read them to each other. For Justin, writing and reading his eulogy to me gave him the final impetus to sever some of the arteries between him and the business. He was able to get in touch with his personal core values while thinking long term. His perception of the purpose of the business changed, and he was able to see it as a means by which to serve him and his personal goals, not for him to serve it. From that moment on, he made a conscience effort to put the business in its place… in line, behind the kids and behind me.

For me, the eulogy exercise uncovered a realization that how *hard* I worked didn't necessarily translate to my overall worth. While my desire to make a positive impact on those around me was partially fulfilled by running a business that employed others, there was far more to this earthly journey than simply working. Even though working is necessary, it doesn't always need to take priority.

I highly encourage you and your spouse to write your own eulogies. It is such a profound experience! Your eulogy should be unapologetically you and deep down the impact you want to make on the world regardless of how large or small your world becomes. In an attempt to challenge you to dig deeply and speak truth, I humbly share the eulogy I wrote when I did this exercise for the first time.

KRISTEN'S EULOGY:

> Kristen became a person who took all the best qualities of her parents and grandparents to become her own intelligent, loving, respected and strong individual. She was always devoted to her projects, whether they be at home or work. It was amazing to see how she successfully balanced herself, her family and her business, neither struggling from her lack of attention.
>
> Kristen was always educating herself, always asking, "Why?" and "How?" She loved to take

things apart and make things with her hands. She was also an excellent hostess and entertainer. She always enjoyed inviting loved ones into her home for good food and fellowship.

She loved adventure, so much so that when her children were in high school, she and Justin were cast on the then popular reality showed called "The Amazing Race"...and they won! That shows only a tidbit of the remarkable marriage she had with Justin. She was strong and active up until the day she died. She always encouraged everyone around her to be their best, physically, mentally and emotionally.

While she will be dearly missed, everyone who had the opportunity to get to know Kristen can take away a warm memory and know that she was completely ready to leave this world, knowing the ones she touched are a little better because of her.

Once we shook off the weight of thinking about our death, we started on the next step toward our vision with an exercise called "Building the Perfect Day." We needed to dream about what our perfect day looked like three years from now. When did we get up? What did we do? Who were we with? Where were we? This exercise proved a little more difficult for me. I think mainly because my idea of a perfect day was so far from what my days looked like at that moment that I could hardly imagine ever getting to my perfect day.

The events I dreamed of happening on a perfect day were not extravagant. I wanted to get up a little before the kids for my morning coffee and quiet reflection time. Then I would get the kids off to school and get ready for the day. I would work for a couple hours and be home when the bus dropped them off in the afternoon. I'd make dinner while they did their homework and then take them to whatever extracurricular activity they were participating in at the time. I would happily work about 20 hours a week, and the rest of the time would be spent keeping the house in order and raising the children. I knew myself well enough to know that if I didn't work at all, I'd go stir crazy. I needed intellectual adult interaction on a regular basis but at the same time, I also craved order and balance at home, and too many hours at the office threw it out of balance. When we were asked to do this exercise, I was experiencing neither order nor balance.

My perfect day wasn't unreasonable from many standards, but it may as well have been to live on Mars. While I felt a vast chasm between me and my perfect day, I look back now and see that it served as a tiny little light at the opening of a deep hole of which I was positioned in the bottom looking up. It was a first step in digging myself back up and into the light.

Unlike the eulogy exercise that forces you to think long-term, dreaming about your perfect day helps you think more short-term.

Give it a try!

Find a quiet place, close your eyes, and take in three long deep breaths. Now, begin to imagine your most ideal day. What time will you wake up? What will be on your agenda for the day? Will you spend time alone? With someone? Who? Where in this wide world will you be? As you ask yourself these questions, pause between each one and visualize your answers. See what it looks like, hear the sounds, smell the aromas, feel the surroundings.

Get creative and know that whatever you want is ok. You can have wants and desires without being greedy. Perhaps your ideal day consists of working for a couple hours a day doing something that you love, and the rest of the day is spent on yourself or your family. Great! Maybe your ideal day is spent lounging by the pool or on a boat in a tropical island sipping mimosas before lunch and switching to piña coladas in the afternoon. Fabulous! Your perfect day could even be getting up before the sun and putting in 12 solid hours at work to be home in time to catch the new episode of CSI. That is great, too! The point here is that this is all about what YOU want, not anyone else but you.

Remember to build what you want your day to look like in three years and know that over time, this will change. Your habits and hobbies will change, develop and evolve. This is to be expected. Do you like to spend your time the same way now as you did when you were in your teens, or twenties? Probably not, so when you are thinking about your perfect day, keep in mind you will be doing this exercise every couple years. Give yourself the freedom to change interests.

Now that we were able to disconnect from our business in order to be able to view it as an extension of us rather than our identity, and we spent some time dreaming about what our perfect day looks like, it was now time to get serious about our personal and business visions.

First, let's talk about personal vision. Through our coaching work, I see this is such an important topic to talk about with your spouse. Assuming your spouse knows what you want without you expressing it can get dangerous—especially when what he or she assumes is wrong! Sitting down with your spouse and having an open conversation about your future and your personal dreams is rich and can yield tremendously powerful results for your future happiness. Hopefully your individual personal dreams will be in line, so you are both running in the same direction and if there are areas that differ, it's great to not be afraid to talk about that, too.

These exercises prompted more open conversations between Justin and me about our future than ever before. Usually we spent our free time talking about the current crisis, but now we were having meaningful discussions about our future and the future of our family. It was difficult at first, especially for me because the previous years of business ownership created a level of cynicism in me that I hated but couldn't deny or quite break free. It was hard to dream about "perfect days" and "business visions" without the accompanying negative thoughts of self-doubt ready to squash these dreams that seemed already so far out of reach.

Confession time: We did our best vision work with a vodka on the rocks for me and a two-finger scotch for Justin. Sometimes that was what it took to be able to disconnect from today just enough to get in touch with tomorrow.

Enough squishy personal stuff—let's get down to business.

Now let's focus on your business vision. Remember that the business and your vision of it should be the vehicle that gets you to your perfect day and ultimately your personal vision. So, the vision that you create for your business needs to act as the foundation or support of those personal dreams. Here are some examples of how a business vision would differ based on your perfect day and personal vision.

Let's say you are the business owner that would like to sit on a yacht, tied to a dock on a tropical island and sip on mimosas and pina coladas all day. Well, that would mean you would need your business to run without your day to day management while generating enough net profit to support your very relaxing lifestyle. You would create your business vision starting from the ultimate goal and work backwards. To support your goals, you'd need to build your business to make, say, $1M a year in net profit. What does your business need to look like to make $1M a year in profit? The answer to that question will be industry specific but as you can see, you can start at the bottom line and work your way up structuring the business around supporting your personal goals and vision.

If we pretend you are the business owner that truly desires to rise before dawn and put in a solid 12 hours at the office every day, it is likely your business vision and structure would look different than the owner that prefers to have other people run the day to day while simply collecting a regular profit check.

The wonderful thing about business and vision is they are all as unique as we are. We can structure a vision however we want. A business structure for one person will not be for all people. That is why it is important to do the work needed to create a vision that is unique to you. When your vision is complete and documented, you start to believe it. This is not an appropriate time to copy and paste something found online (never mind the possibility of plagiarism). The vision comes from within you. It is your heart, and your heart is different than every other business owner.

For a vision to be well rounded, here are some things it should address.

- What will be the size of the business in terms of sales, net profit, number of customers, number of employees?
- What services or products will you sell?
- Where will you sell the products or provide the service?
- What will be your role in the company?
- What will your company culture be?
- What will your community reputation and involvement be?

You will create two versions of your vision. The full out, no-holds-barred, goal setting vision will be your strategic vision. This version will address every aspect of what your business will look like in 3-5 years including sales and net profit goals, how much you want the business to support you financially, all the nitty gritty details.

The second version will be the motivational version. This version will omit any personal financial information—or anything you wouldn't want to share with your employees—because...

Once your vision is complete, you will share it with your employees—the motivational version. What better way to unite employees within a company than to show them what they are all working for? When they can all see the vision of the company, then their decisions will be shaped in such a way as to move toward the vision. True synergy is achieved when the company values align with the personal values of its employees. An added and sometimes unexpected side effect of sharing the motivation vision with your team: rotten apples will organically weed themselves out, which is not a bad thing. It's similar to the metaphor of the bus. "This is the bus, and this is where it's going. If you don't want to go there, then you're welcome to get off at the station because we are fixin' to be rollin' out."

Here in the southeastern part of the United States, college football is huge. Everyone has their favorite team and is fiercely loyal whether they attended that team's college or not. Even if the team has a season with no wins or several seasons with no wins, the fans are still supportive. They wear the team hats and shirts; they put team stickers on their cars and flags on their front porches. You can pick out fans of your team in a crowd and can easily strike up a conversation with them about the team this year or how they became fans in the first place. A vision inspired by the personal values of its owners can create the same comradery among employees as a pig skin in a 120-yard field can do among fans.

KRISTEN

There came a day, once our vision was finally fully drafted, when we presented it to the employees. Justin and I had worked so hard and were incredibly proud of the words we had organized on this paper. It was a culmination of our two personal sets of values infused into a future business we could finally get excited about. Our business coach gave her final stamp of approval on our creation and let us know it was time to share it with the team. I stood in front of the room and read our vision aloud. They didn't know what we were going to say; most of them didn't even know we were working on this. Hell, some of them didn't even know what a vision was. But I read it anyway and as I read the last three words on the paper in my hands, I looked around the room. Those that had been with us for a long time were touched, I even saw a tear or two. Not necessarily because of the words that I spoke but more because they could hear and feel my passion. I could see a breath of fresh air being blown into that room and on that day, there was a one-degree shift. I know one degree doesn't seem like a lot of movement but from where we were, it was forward movement in the right direction and that was enough motivation to keep going.

Your business vision is a living and breathing document in your organization. It is not meant to be written and stuffed in a desk drawer never again to see the light of day. We've created a worksheet on our website, www.businessspouse.com, that will guide you through creating your vision statement. A curated version of your vision, aside from the strategic and motivation version you already made, can be created to share with customers via marketing material like your website. I doubt you would want to share sales and profit goals with your customers, but they could buy into the portion of your vision that illustrates core values and competitive advantage. You are not changing the content of your vision to show your customers, simply thinning it out, keeping only the sections that pertain to them.

A truthful and well written vision can be used for marketing and recruiting material. We attract applicants with similar core values by using verbiage from our vision right in the ad. When we ask applicants why they applied for a job at our company, we often hear them speak to the ad and how they connected with it more so than any other ad they had seen. That's usually a good sign the values between the company and the applicant are aligned.

Because your vision will be alive and well in your business, it's important to understand that it will change over time. When you start to see that you have met more than half of the goals laid out within the current vision or you are nearing your first three-year mark, then it's time to update. Imagine in three more years what you'll want your business to look like. Will it be bigger? Smaller? Will you offer the same services? Will you participate in the same capacity as you do now? Look at each section of the vision and think about how it might change between now and then. Re-write, redistribute, and revitalize and always keep your vision at the forefront of decision making within your business. Having a vision is like having a target to shoot for. When you are laser-focused on your target, you can move towards it with the precision of a sniper.

Here was the version of the vision we painstakingly created:

At AGS Installations we strive to set ourselves apart from our competition with **excellent quality of service** *and exceptional employees. We are 'plumbing professionals' in all senses of the word. Plumbing professionals are* **knowledgeable, friendly, clean** *and* **passionate** *about making sure our customers will give us a "Perfect 10" in a survey. We aim to outdo the plumber/service contractor stereotype with every phone call and every visit to a customer's home or business.*

Our employees are **thoroughly trained** *in our trade and our specific processes. AGS Installations technicians are clean cut, uniformly dressed, happy employees and that image projects from them during every encounter with customers. All of our* *employees* **respect** *our customers' time and property as if it were their own and our technicians take great care to leave the job site clean and in better repair than it was upon their arrival. Our* **organized, efficient, systematic** *approach to every job, in the office and in the field, from creation to completion, ensures we are* **providing our very best every time**.

Our employees' level of **pride** *and* **confidence** *in their team shows through in their actions and proves, beyond our technical ability, why we are the* **best in our industry**. *In order to promote our culture of* **ownership, pride** *and* **confidence** *our employees hold the same or similar values as the business and its owners.*

AGS Installations strives to promote a culture of **happy** *employees by ensuring the right people are in the right places, they have the tools to complete their job to the best of their ability and they are* **rewarded** *for taking* **ownership** *of their position and "getting the job done right…the first time."*

Justin and I worked with a pair of married entrepreneurs who started a business repairing and selling attachments for heavy earth moving equipment. Their business was sparked by the ever popular notion that what they were doing as employees for another company could be done more efficiently and for more money out on their own.

It didn't take long before they found themselves in the middle of multiple spinning plates: customers, suppliers and employees all needed their attention, and each day they were fighting the fires of the business with no clear direction.

I listened to the wife one day early in their business development as she vented about how her husband, who was also her business partner, didn't know—or at least wouldn't share with her—what he envisioned for the future of their business. She knew the importance of having a vision for direction and was frustrated that he wouldn't take the time to think about the future. She really just wanted some reassurance that there was a goal, a light at the end of the tunnel they were digging.

I am friends with this couple on social media and during the year following our conversations about vision, I watched as their business began to thrive and as a result, their personal lives. I caught up with them several months later and asked her how their vision was coming along. She shared that her husband finally came around and got clear on a vision for the company. She said now they are both working toward the same goals, and making business decisions is far easier when you ask yourself if the opportunity gets you closer to your vision. She and her husband's act of getting clear on their vision didn't solve every issue they were facing at the time; however, it was a huge step forward, and it got the momentum moving forward toward success.

CHAPTER 3

Take the Clock by the Hands

"Either you own your time or your time owns you." —Justin Deese

"The bad news is time flies. The good news is you're the pilot." —Michael Althsuler

How often have you said in exasperation, "There aren't enough hours in the day!"

We have always been taught that being busy is good. Even in elementary school our teachers gave us *busy* work which taught us from an early age that if we weren't doing something, then we weren't being productive. This behavior of being busy followed us to adulthood, and it tagged along right behind when we became business owners. If being busy meant we were being productive, and being productive meant being successful, then couldn't we eliminate the middleman and just say being busy meant being successful?

Kristen and I fell into that trap from the very beginning of our lives as entrepreneurs. We were beyond busy. On a typical day, I was up at 5am, on the days that I could actually sleep that is. Half the time I'd wake up at 2am, not be able to go back to sleep so I'd crack open the laptop to start working on some of the things that I didn't manage to get done the day before.

I'd bury myself in the mile-long list of things that needed my attention all day long. Most of the time I survived on coffee and one meal a day. I would get so immersed in the day-to-day fires that needed to be put out that I'd skip breakfast and work right through lunch. Before I knew it, dinner time arrived, my stomach would finally yell louder than the to-do list, and I would find myself rummaging through the fridge eating whatever I could find with one hand while making myself dinner with the other. The evening activities would come and go. Sometimes I would try to participate, but my phone or laptop would get the best of my attention. It always seemed like there was some kind of crisis that needed an immediate resolution. Weekends, holidays, birthdays, vacations—the business didn't care what day of the year it was, and we didn't know any different. We thought that this is what owning a business meant, working all the time because if we were busy, then we'd eventually get to the point of successful.

Our business coach knew and understood what we were going through, and she also knew that if she didn't teach us some time management techniques that we would not be able to absorb and implement the other valuable lessons she was encouraging us to learn. Like a sponge dripping with water, there was no room to soak up more water until we took the time to squeeze out the extra.

Justin and I were both operating in a constant state of over-whelm, but neither of us realized time management had anything to do with it. From our coach, we learned that effective time management is one the of the most crucial skills requiring mastery in order to have a successful business, marriage and fulfilling life. In general, we put more effort into managing money than time and in many cases, even our effort to manage money was weak and arguably nonexistent.

We have 24 hours in the day just like everyone else. We are all working within those strict boundaries. Yet how is it that some people are running around with their hair on fire, always late and overbooked, and others have it all under control with a list of crossed off items and a feeling of accomplishment at the end of each day?

We worked with our business coach for nearly two years and over the course of our time together, there were a handful of guiding principles that seemed to show themselves often— sometimes to our advantage and sometimes working against us. There were many times that we figured out the hard way that we just needed to get out of our own way! It was our own limiting beliefs that stood between us and success.

We have compiled a couple of these paradigms we picked up along the way. These are the simple phrases that were powerful enough to strike a nerve and shift our perspective a few degrees. The first paradigm is the concept that our business was a reflection of us.

Let that sink in for a moment.

> *Your business is a reflection of you—how you do one thing is how you do everything.*

That one hit particularly hard for me. I first read about it in *The E-Myth* by Michael Gerber, but like so many things before, just because I heard it didn't mean I was listening. Was our coach telling us that this business is jacked up right now because we are jacked up?

When she said this, our first instinct was to defend ourselves. That's not true, we'd say. This business is jacked up because our employees acted entitled, were ungrateful, couldn't make a decision to save their lives, and our customers always want something for nothing. We have to fight for every penny we get from them. She would patiently wait for us to take a breath between rebuttals and show us each time how the outward problem we were experiencing was merely a symptom of an inward limiting belief or weakness we were facing. *Your business is a reflection of you,* she would calmly say, time and time again.

The concept that our business is a reflection of us showed up clearly in our time management techniques before coaching. Kristen and I didn't respect our own time, so our employees didn't respect our time (or theirs) either. We were unorganized and therefore attracted unorganized chaos. Our time management techniques, before we learned otherwise, consisted of waiting until the very last minute to complete a project and the only reason we'd even have a deadline is if an outside party placed one on us. We certainly didn't place any deadline on ourselves—that looked too much like personal accountability and it was much easier to blame other things that took advantage of our time and prevented us from meeting that internal goal of a deadline.

When something wasn't completed on time the default answer was, "I didn't have time." This leads us to the second paradigm that we learned and are now sharing with you.

> *You have a choice on how to spend your time, and your choices up until now have gotten you here.*

Again, Kristen and I pushed back. Nope, we said, definitely not true for us. During our early years of entrepreneurship we wholeheartedly believed that we were forced into the decisions we had made to get us where we were and that what we chose to spend our time on was only decided because that issue was calling the loudest for our attention. The squeaky wheel gets the grease; we had no other choice.

And again, our coach would patiently and calmly hold up the proverbial mirror and remind us that we did indeed have a choice every time we were presented with an issue, and the choices we made in the past got us to the present state. Yes, there are times when things happen that are truly out of our control, but we still have a choice in the aftermath of the unexpected. At a bare minimum for those things that happen that are truly out of our control, our choice lies in our reaction.

She gave a couple of examples of this concept of choice— at the time they seemed extreme but now that we fully understand and embody this principle, it makes total sense. A common misconception that many people believe is that we are *forced* to make certain decisions, or we *had to* do certain things. This is simply not the case. Everything we do every day is a choice. We choose to pay the mortgage rather than live on the streets; we choose to pay the utility bill so we can have electricity and heat. These are both choices with positive outcomes. There are things we choose to do that have negative outcomes as well. Maybe we choose to smoke or drink instead of choosing meditation or exercise to relieve stress. Or we choose to work late at the office to get a few more things on our task list done instead of going home and spending time with the rest of the family. The options we choose bring us here. We choose to spend time on the things that are important to us, or the things that call the loudest for our attention. We choose to fill our time with tasks rather than spending time working on the larger vision of our business. Of course, things are going to happen that are beyond our control; however, *that* choice lies in our response.

The next paradigm seems overly simple, but sometimes it's the simplicity that allows it to be overlooked and allows us to get overbooked.

> *Saying, "Yes," to one thing means you are saying, "No," to something else.*

Not only as business owners but as humans, Justin and I had a habit of overcommitting ourselves which in itself can lead to overwhelm and burn out, so when this idea was presented to us, our response was less push back and denial and more, "Oohhhh, that makes sense..."

When you say, "Yes," to something, you have effectively said, "No," to something else. For example, perhaps you said, "Yes," to hitting the snooze button three times on the alarm clock this morning and by doing so, you effectively said, "No," to getting a workout in to start your day. There's a pretty good chance that as you blindly fumbled around your nightstand to silence the alarm, your conscious brain probably said, "I am so tired. I don't feel like getting up."

Subconsciously what your brain really meant was, "I refuse to work out this morning." You said, "No," to getting up and working out whether you realized it or not. The trick here is to be aware of the opposite side of the commitment and take accountability for what you just said, "No," to.

This same concept can be applied to money as well. Maybe you said, "Yes," to buying a new piece of equipment for your business and by doing so, you said, "No," to putting that money into the company Christmas party fund you wanted to keep in the budget. Or you spent money to get your nails done every week instead of saving it or spending it on the vacation you are planning.

When presented with a decision regarding time or money, ask yourself this question: if I say, "Yes," to this, what will I be saying no to? The answer will not always be negative, but understanding this concept is important when it comes to evaluating with what you are filling your time.

Ok, moving on. This next one was a little mind blowing.

Effective multi-tasking is a myth.

As a business owner, you have probably read through countless resumes trying to decode the applicants' lists of strengths neatly bulleted on the page. Undoubtedly, most resumes' description of administrative skill includes a phrase similar to this: "Organized, efficient and excellent at multi-tasking." I'd like to take a moment to myth-bust that last word.

To claim you are a multi-tasker is not actually a great asset. You see, it is impossible for the brain to concentrate on more than one thing with 100% focus on both. Have you ever been in the car in an unfamiliar place and found yourself turning down the radio so you could focus on where you were going? This is because your brain sees the radio as a distraction and in order to give the more important task of driving your 100% undivided attention, you feel better when you remove the distraction by turning down the radio.

There is a reason texting and driving at the same time are becoming illegal—sure you can do both at the same time—but it's risky and the consequences of trying to multi-task in this scenario can be catastrophic! So, to be fair, you can technically do more than one thing at a time, but how well are you performing each task individually?

This concept is applied in business by understanding that we are much more efficient and accurate when we work on one project or task at a time. Multi-tasking leads to mistakes; however, for many business owners, sharpening this skill of true focus takes much time and effort. It is so easy to be distracted and tempted to try to do more than one thing at a time. This is so true for Justin—he's got ADD. Not only was he always easily distracted, but he felt like there was so much he needed to do on any given day that the only way he could get it all done was to multi-task.

It might even sound counterproductive to *not* multi-task when practicing good time management skills; however, in the long run it's less costly to give 100% to one thing at a time than it is to give 25% to four things simultaneously.

Once our business coach got us to fully understand these four principles, she was able to introduce to us the first step in getting control of our time. On one particular call, she sent us a time tracking log and asked us to write down everything we did and what time we started the task on the log. We were also supposed to document distractions and interruptions. Very much like a food diary except with minutes rather than calories. To Justin this felt like busy work, and he was already busy enough. He didn't need the extra work, nor did he even know how he was going to find the time to write down everything he did.

This was one of the times during coaching that even though we couldn't see the point of the exercise just yet, we had to trust the process. Certainly, there had to be a good reason we were asked to write everything down knowing that task in itself was incredibly time consuming and even on the verge of annoying.

We reluctantly did what we were asked to do, and every day for a week we wrote down everything that we did because we needed a baseline of how our time was being spent. Similar to a dietician asking for a food diary, she needed to know—and she needed us to see—what was happening during the course of a day. What time we got up, what time we started working, what we worked on, who disrupted us for what reason and how long—we documented it all. After that, she had us go through and analyze how we had spent our time for the week.

In general, Kristen is more organized and focused than I am. Keeping a time log for a week was not my favorite thing to do, but after I had several days documented, I could look at how my day unfolded right in front of me—the words on my page written in my own handwriting. There was no denying the information on those pages because I was the one that put them there.

I sat at my desk in amazement as I looked at what I had written for the past week. There were so many things on that list, most lasting less than 10 minutes, tons of distractions—no wonder I never felt like I was making any headway on my ever-growing list of stuff to get done! I didn't necessarily think I had bad time management skills before, but this exercise served as a spotlight on all the holes in my boat. All those holes filled my boat with water and were enough to bring me down below the surface. These logs spelled out right in front of me all the stupid little things I was getting wrapped up in and allowing to consume my entire day. Like a smoker who had no idea how much they were spending on cigarettes until they started counting the dollars, I was oblivious to the amount of time I was spending on things I had no business being in the middle of. Not only did it show what I was doing, it showed me what I wasn't doing as well. Nowhere on that log had I spent any time on my vision, employee development, my health, my kids or my marriage.

That was another turning point for me. I could immediately see what tasks I was doing that needed to be delegated, and I knew I needed to focus on creating a list of the tasks I needed to *stop* doing along with a list of tasks I needed to *start* doing if I was ever going to get control of my time.

Here are some things to keep an eye out for when reviewing your day:

- Are you bouncing from one thing to the next every few minutes, or are you diligently working on one thing at a time until it's finished?

- How many times are you interrupted by a distraction like a phone call, employee question, social media, or email notification?
- How long does it take you to get refocused after the distraction?
- How much of your time is spent doing things other employees should be doing?
- How much of your time is spent on strategic work versus tactical tasks?

What do your time logs tell you about your day? How are you spending your time? Is there a time during the day when your brain functions better and you can focus? Are you jumping from task to task but never actually getting anything done?

Now that you can see on paper right in front of you how your day unfolds, you can make a conscious decision every day to take control of your time—rather than your list of *to-dos* controlling you. You won't have control every single day, but sometimes simply becoming aware fuels unconscious improvement.

Here are some things you can implement right away to see an immediate difference in what you can get done in less time than it has taken before.

- **Use your calendar**—Refrain from jotting down appointments and things to do on post-it notes and junk mail envelopes and actually use your calendar. Schedule everything, not just dentist appointments and webinars. Some examples of what we'd expect to see on a business owner's calendar are meetings, team training, daily strategic time, task list time, and email time.

- **Batch like activities**—Schedule outgoing phone calls back to back, only check mail during scheduled times and schedule employee meetings back to back. For some people it takes time to get into the appropriate mind frame for each type of task. You can reduce the amount of time spent preparing yourself for one task by batching all the similar tasks into one time block.

- **Implement daily 1-hour business development meetings with your inner entrepreneur**—This time is set aside for dreaming. We learned by reading E-Myth by Michael Gerber that your inner entrepreneur, (you know, the one that convinced you it would be a good idea to start your own business) has gotten squashed by your inner technician who has been working *in* the business. Your inner entrepreneur needs uninterrupted, non-pressured time to come up with the great ideas needed to propel you towards your vision. This might be tough at first, especially since your inner technician will be impatiently tapping his foot and reminding you that you have a TON of stuff to do today, but simply thank that technician for his or her service and give him a break for a little bit. The technician focuses on micro while the entrepreneur focuses on the macro.

  Coaching should be approached with the inner entrepreneur. While the inner technician may be capable of implementing some of the tasks presented during coaching to see some positive changes in the business, he will really only stay busy patching holes. The inner entrepreneur on the other hand will be able to use the tools provided to make the vision come alive. The technician can only see that there is a hole in the boat and will go to work patching the hole. The entrepreneur will take a higher vantage point and see that the hole came from the shallow water and pointed rocks hidden below the surface. Then he'll patch the hole and steer the ship to deeper waters to avoid the same problem in the future.

- **Schedule hard tasks during your strongest part of the day**—We all have parts of the day when we have more focus and energy. Use this time to your advantage and schedule the hard stuff for those times. My strongest part of the day is from 6:30am to 11am. As a matter of fact, the majority of this book was written between those hours of the day. We all have certain things that we feel are more difficult to do than others. Perhaps it's a phone call you need to make to an unhappy customer or a difficult conversation you are anticipating with an employee. Or maybe the hardest part of your day is the time you need to set aside to work strategically on your business. Maybe the hardest part for you is analyzing and understanding your numbers or working on your marketing plan. I think you get the point—pick what's hard for you and do it during the part of the day when your brain is firing on all cylinders. Why would you expect yourself to do amazingly well on a difficult task if you are tired, hungry or overly distracted? Don't put that much pressure on yourself, and leverage your energy and times of strong focus to your advantage.

- **Minimize distractions**—Close your door. If this is something you are not comfortable doing, then get comfortable with it. If you work in a shared office space, figure out how to get quiet time, alone time. For a multitude of reasons including employee development and strategic thinking, as the business owner, you must have a place where and a time when you can be uninterrupted. There are times during the day when having the door open is appropriate but definitely not during your one hour of business development or when you are working on your task list. I think as leaders of our business, we feel that if we close our door, we are isolating ourselves from the rest of the employees that are doing our work. We think they will resent the fact that our door is closed and think we are too good to be in the trenches with them—or worse yet— maybe we are talking about them! Not to worry, a closed door handled in the right way can nip those negative feelings in the bud and be presented in a very positive light—because it is a good thing!
Invite your employees to book a 15 minute appointment on your calendar if they need something while your door is closed. Reassure everyone that you are not avoiding them; you simply need some uninterrupted time during the day to work on the business, and if they need you for something, they can schedule a time to meet with you. If you use an electronic calendar which I highly recommend, share it with your employees. They don't have to see exactly what's scheduled if you don't want them to. You can make the setting only show busy and free

time. Allow them to drop a 15-minute meeting on your calendar to discuss what they were tempted to knock on your door for. During the meeting give them your undivided attention so they learn that hanging on to their question until the meeting can give them the reward of your complete focus.

By implementing this calendar policy, you will likely find that many of the small questions you get asked throughout the day will get solved by the employees because they didn't want to wait until you were free for a solution. Don't become a complete recluse locked in your office with the door closed all the time. Make sure it's open sometimes and when it is, employees are free to come in, have a seat and chat. Not only does this help minimize distractions, it is actually a nice way to set some boundaries with your employees and we'll talk more about boundaries in a later chapter.

Ok, we're changing gears a little bit but still talking about minimizing distractions. Rather than checking your email every time you hear your phone or laptop chime, schedule two or three 30-minute blocks of email time throughout the day and turn off the email notifications on your phone and computer.

Email is an important form of communication in business these days, and we have been conditioned to expect a response to an email almost as quickly as if we were having a face to face conversation. The thought of only checking and responding to emails a couple times a day may seem impossible but just like you have conditioned your contacts to get an immediate response, you can condition them to now wait a moment. It might take a little while to retrain them and for issues that really do need your immediate attention, you should provide another form of communication. Perhaps for people outside of the company you can provide your office number that is answered by a receptionist. For our employees we used inner-office communication tools like Skype if a response is needed quickly. Here's the deal with that though—when your door is closed, your Skype should be on *do not disturb* so your employees aren't going around the closed door electronically for your attention.

- Here's how to handle your inbox during your scheduled email time. Starting with the oldest email first, read it and decide if your response or the action the author is asking you to take can be completed in less than two minutes. If yes, then knock it out. If the response or action will take longer than two minutes, place it on your task list and move on to the next email. Follow this procedure until you have checked each new email. If you still have time left of your allotted email time, then you can go back to work on the items you had to move from your inbox to your task list. But if your email time is over, then those items should wait and be completed during the time you have allotted to work on your task list.

- I know what you are thinking—if I moved my emails from my inbox to my task list, then my task list would get longer before I have the opportunity to get anything done. Before you spend too much time protesting email time, keep in mind the 80/20 rule. This suggestion can work 80% of the time—sometimes stuff needs to get handled now—but know the difference between a forest fire and a controlled burn.

- Last thing on minimizing distractions and then we'll move on. Turn off social media notifications *gasp* - yes, I said it. If social media is an important part of your day, then schedule time for it on your calendar as well. When it's not social media time, put your phone away to avoid being tempted to pick it up and scroll through your news feed. There are many companies these days that legitimately conduct business through social media and if that's you, then rock on. Again, awareness is the key here—if you are allowing the news feed on your Facebook and Instagram account to take up too much of the time that you should be working on your business, then put it down.

Here are a few more tips and tricks for managing your time:

- Break big projects up into manageable bites—there are lots of project management apps out there to help with this.
- Don't overbook yourself—leave some free time and gaps on your schedule whenever possible. Sometimes appointments run over, things pop up that must be done, and you need to make sure there is some

reserve time built into your schedule to handle those things with grace.

- Start with higher priority tasks—this is kind of a no brainer, but I felt the need to say it anyway. Take the time to prioritize your tasks and work them in order even if the one you really want to do is on the bottom of the list.

- Delegate if you have employees to delegate to and if you don't have employees, then outsource when it economically makes sense. One way to decide what to delegate would be to ask yourself: how much per hour would you pay someone else to do this specific task? If the answer is "not a lot, it doesn't take a very specific skill set to complete this task," then it should probably be delegated. As the business owner your time is very valuable—don't waste it performing lower paying tasks if you have the resources and manpower to delegate, thus freeing up your time for higher level tasks and thoughts.

- Set deadlines with yourself and for those you have delegated to. Here's the kicker on this one—keep the set deadline!

- Don't take work home—when you are home focus on your family and your selfcare, so you are rested and refreshed when you go back to work the next day.

- Use gatekeepers.

- Don't procrastinate—*Eat That Frog* by Brian Tracy is a good read on procrastination.

- Don't skip meals, but don't overeat at lunch. We don't talk about food and nutrition very much in this book, but it is so powerfully important for our overall performance as human beings. When we skip meals, overeat or make unhealthy food choices, we are making our body physically work harder to get the nutrition it needs, and there is less energy left for our brain. As business owners we need our brains to work hard, so we need to fuel it accordingly.

- Teach time management skills to your employees. This is huge! Many of the things you learn through-out this book can be taught to your employees as well—that's why we call it "employee development." It's our duty as the leaders of our organizations to help our employees learn and grow both profes-sionally and personally. Let's face it, our employees won't work for us forever—we don't want them too! We want them to make a positive impact on our lives, allow us to make a positive impact on theirs, grow, become better and move on to the next step of their journey in this world. Lead, coach, mentor, grow, cultivate, harvest and when it's time, set them free.

- Audit your own time management skills from time to time. We all slack or fall off the wagon every now and then. Sometimes it's a gradual slide off the back, and sometimes we fall right off and land on our heads. It's ok, when we find ourselves slipping, go back to basics; locate the weak spot and give it the time and attention it's calling for.

Time management does not come easy to many people, and it is something that you will more than likely need to work on, evaluate and work on some more. One telltale sign that your time management skills may have been abandoned is when the feeling of overwhelm begins to creep back in. When this happens, reread this guide and reimplement what you have learned here. And of course, if that doesn't relieve the feeling of overwhelm, reach out to your coach for help.

Time is a nonrenewable resource, unlike money which can be replenished if lost, once time is gone it's gone. Considering the preciousness of time, wouldn't it behoove us all to make the best of each and every day, hour, and minute?

CHAPTER 4

Setting and Sticking to Clearly Defined Roles

"Just like on the road, if you don't stay in your lane, accidents are more likely to occur." —Justin Deese

"You do you…and only you."—Kristen Deese

JUSTIN

Like many small businesses run by husband and wife partners, we did not start out with clearly defined, well organized, well thought out roles. For the first year or two I wore most of the hats of the business. I was the salesman, the account manager, the technician, and the marketer. I made sure the customers and vendors were happy and the company was in compliance with the local jurisdictions. I ordered the tools and equipment required to complete the jobs, I answered all the incoming calls for the company morning, noon, and night and when the time came, I hired, trained and managed our first employee.

I recognized very early that as the visionary and entrepreneur, these tasks in no way made me happy, content or fulfilled. But all of the tasks had to be done and being the only full-time employee of the company and the only one generating any income, I didn't have a choice but to fill all of those roles. If we'd had an organizational chart, which of course we did not, it would have looked like:

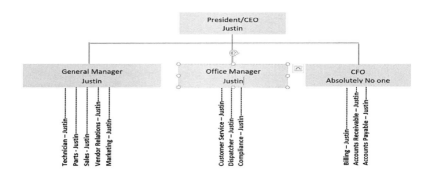

Forward progress followed a very herky-jerky flow caused by the fact that I am only one person and the swing from one major role to another meant a complete mindset shift. I would spend a couple days a week being the technician so that money would be coming in the business. But then I needed to generate more sales opportunities and networking connections and I couldn't do that with stained up work clothes and dirty hands, so the sales tasks couldn't be done on the same day as the technician tasks. This meant that the technician tasks (that part that generated cash) needed to come to a screeching halt while I was out there, feet on the street, in slacks, dress shoes and a snazzy polo with *my* company logo stitched on the front left side generating sales connections.

I'd make some good connections, get some new leads; meanwhile, there were customers who needed their appliances installed, so I'd have to stop the sales role, remove the sales uniform, put the work uniform back on and go install appliances. This meant the warm sales leads I had just spent the time generating were becoming cooler by the minute.

The other tasks I needed to do to move this business forward were sprinkled in all over the place. There was always a logistical aspect of scheduling and routing that needed to be done which took me away from both the technical work (generating immediate cash) AND the outside sales role (generating new business- filling the pipeline). It was a vicious cycle, and it became apparent pretty quickly that I would never be able to scale this business if I didn't bring others in to help.

At first, Kristen helped when she could. She was already working a full-time job managing an upscale hair salon in a bustling suburb of Atlanta, so her help was only available in the evenings and on weekends. In those hours, thanks to the fact that she had an accounting degree meant that she would do the invoicing and gather and organize some of the paperwork. Basically, she would do the things that I just simply did not have the capacity to do nor the wish to learn to do. I was happy to hand any tasks to her that had anything to do with numbers and the seemingly infinite fine detail that went along with the tasks that needed to be done to keep the books up to date. In the beginning I wasn't quite sure what "the books" meant, but it sounded daunting and well out of my wheelhouse.

It was also an added layer of reassurance knowing that the person watching the money was my wife. I didn't have to worry about whether the bookkeeper was spooning the cream off the top because of who the person in charge of the cash was.

Throughout our time in the small business world and business coaching we have seen countless scenarios just like ours. The husband starts out as the technician and the wife, many times with previous accounting experience, ends up assuming the role of bookkeeper and administrative assistant. Many times, it happens without real meaningful discussion or a plan - almost like an unspoken rule - it just makes sense. Maybe it's because she is more detail-oriented and organized, or maybe she has more patience to do the research needed to figure out a bookkeeping issue, and it might even be that it's something that she can do in between all her other responsibilities of being a wife or mother or career woman or all of those at once. Regardless of the reason why, this first organizational chart of a young business in the home services industry consisting of the husband running the day to day and the wife managing the money and administrative tasks is an extremely popular early business layout—and could likely apply to you as well.

KRISTEN

Initially this layout worked okay for Justin and me. I often joked that Justin would be out all day rustling stuff up, and I'd come home after my day at work and get everything that he rustled cleaned up behind him. This was the time in our life when our son was very young, and our daughter wasn't born yet. Because Zack was an infant, his bedtime was early, and I would get a couple hours of work done between his bedtime and mine. My main responsibility was getting the invoices for the jobs completed that day over to the customer for payment, but that was just the tip of the iceberg in terms of the other things that consumed my evening time and filled up the list of things I wanted to implement in the company. Seems like every day there was a new system or process or form that needed to be created to make tasks easier. Plus, there were reports and calculations that I wanted to watch on a regular basis but never could find the time to do so. As much as I knew these things would help us, I simply didn't have the time or capacity to do the extra things I saw a need for in the few tired hours of the day I could contribute.

Soon, discussions of me leaving my job to come work for the company full-time became more and more frequent. Justin's brain operates like a chess game—he is always thinking three moves out. For him the obvious next step needed to propel the business forward was to have me in there full-time. The administrative and accounting department was becoming a bottleneck for the business, and he wasn't equipped to train, (nor could we afford) to hire another employee to take on this role.

In my mind, the fear far outweighed the excitement of that decision. One of my main fears was the anticipated lack of adult human interaction. My need for this adult human face to face connection was a driving factor for going back to work after my son was born. I needed that time spent with adults, having adult conversations, listening to adult music, eating adult food. There was only so much Thomas the Train and smashed bananas that I could handle without becoming desperate for adult stimulation. I wanted to believe I would get that stimulation from Justin, but we knew by now the reality of running a business. Justin was always working, usually on job sites and when he was home, the conversations always revolved around the business.

There was also the fact that I loved my job at the salon. I was good at what I did, I enjoyed working with my female colleagues, and I looked forward to seeing and talking to the different clients—even the tough ones. It gave me an avenue to serve, and I loved making the clients smile. Not only was I worried about how I would replace the source of the adult interaction if I worked from home, but I also worried that I would lose the identity I was building at the salon.

And of course, I worried about the financial impact that leaving a full-time job could have if we weren't able to generate that lost personal income through the business. My check from the salon was by no means enough to cover all of our personal bills, but it was income from an outside source. Taking that away—putting the last of our eggs into this business Justin had created put a new and much deeper level of accountability to make this business work on our shoulders. After all, it wasn't just the two of us anymore; we now had to consider how our decisions could potentially affect our son.

I eventually made the leap from the salon to the appliance installation business and took on the role as the book-keeper. At that point in our business, there were three appliance installation trucks, including Justin, making installs on a regular basis, and there was one customer service woman taking calls and scheduling customers. The basement of our house had been transformed into a bonified administrative department. It was equipped with four phone lines, a dedicated fax machine that seemed to be sending or receiving non-stop and three distinct desk spaces. We were accepting jobs from more retail stores by the week, and soon our service span covered the entire metro Atlanta area. We were so busy that I didn't have time to worry about all the things I was worried about before I left the security of the salon.

Justin and I have always done a pretty good job of *staying in our lanes* as he likes to call it. We both knew each other's strengths and weaknesses, and it was assumed that Justin would handle the relationship development, and I would handle behind the scenes organization. We were lucky our skills were complementary and both excited to be working within our own unique abilities.

When I work with clients now, one of the first things I ask is what role they serve in the business and whether that is the role they truly want to play. I have talked to several clients in a similar situation that Justin and I were in, facing the overwhelm head on, and have found that many of them are assuming the other is playing the role they are playing because they *want* to. Or worse yet, one spouse is experiencing feelings of anger because the other is meddling in or undermining their role in front of the rest of the company. In my experience, it was usually the wife that is the meddler offering unsolicited advice to the husband on how to improve. In all instances she meant well but she was clearly stepping out of her lane. As a coach, it is my job to hold up the mirror and gently show the offending party the traffic infraction and offer guidance on how to be heard without stepping into the wrong lane. Often, I'll facilitate an open conversation between the couple and one (or both) will discover something they didn't know about each other before. Sometimes there are also feelings of distress that arise, and when we spend the time to peel back the layers, we find the distress is caused by an underlying lack of communication which we will discuss in great detail later in the book.

I worked with a client that owns a mid-sized plumbing company which has been in the family for generations. One day I called his office number at our scheduled time, and he answered the phone in a complete panic. I could hear immediately in his voice that he was in crisis mode and as soon as I asked how he was doing, he unloaded the entire story of his situation. What it boiled down to was that his office manager of over 20 years announced her resignation just prior to our call.

Not only was he shocked that she was leaving, but he had no idea how he was going to find someone to train to do her job. She had been doing so much for the business, and he completely relied on her to handle everything, so her resignation came as a strong blow to the side of the head for him.

He shared that his wife had offered to help take over the office manager role during the interim while he located and trained a replacement. I asked him what he thought about her offering to step up and temporarily plug that hole. I also asked him if his wife would be a good fit as the office manager on a long-term basis. He hadn't thought of that as an option but also didn't think it was a bad idea either.

"What role, if any, would your wife like to play within the company?" I asked him. There was a long pause on the other end of the line.

"Well, I don't think she wants to be the office manager" he said and paused again, "but I guess I don't really know," he added timidly.

"Have you ever asked her?" I said gently.

"No. I haven't."

I could hear the impact of that simple question through the quiet space. He couldn't answer that question, and he didn't know the answer because he had never bothered to ask her. Remember earlier when I said they had been working together for over twenty years? I sent him off with some work to do after that call. He was to sit down with his wife (who was also his business partner) and have an open conversation about where she saw herself in the company.

On our next call, he expressed that a weight had been lifted off his shoulders.

"So," I said, "how did the conversation go with your wife?"

"It went really well!" he gushed. "It turns out she actually wants to be the permanent, fulltime office manager. I can honestly say, I didn't see that coming but I am so relieved that she wants to take on this job. Now I don't have to worry about recruiting, hiring and training a new employee."

What a huge revelation for them both. And it was all because he asked his wife one simple question: what do you want to do in this company?

While this client story demonstrates the importance of having an open line of communication with your business partner spouse…of which we will dig deeper in chapter 5…it also illustrates what can happen when assumptions are made about the roles that each of you play with in the business. Having clearly defined roles, capitalizing on one another's strengths, and having open communication about wants, desires, likes and dislikes can save your business many headaches as you grow and develop. It is important to list and document your roles as business owners.

This next section will help set up those clearly defined roles and get them on paper. In order to know where you are going you first need to find out where you are so the best place to start is with listing the tasks you currently do. This exercise should be completed separately first and then afterwards you and your spouse should discuss your lists. A pdf version of this form can be found on our website, www.businessspouse.com.

Date		
Current Tasks	Keep or Delegate	Why?
Future Tasks	Keep of Delegate	Why?

This exercise can be a great inventory of what you are doing in your business, whether you like to do it or not and what you might rather be doing instead. The first step will be to date your worksheet. (We recommend that you keep the exercises that you complete throughout this book so that you can reflect on them in the future. Doing this serves as wonderful opportunities to review how far you have come and what you have accomplished over time.)

After you have dated your worksheet, you'll list all the tasks you do now. Once you have done that, you add any tasks you would like to do that you currently are not. And here comes the fun part—next to each item on the currently doing list, note whether you want to keep doing it or you'd rather have someone else do it and the reason why. And finally, next to each of the things on your future task list write down why you want to do those.

We added the reflection question of reasoning to this worksheet because of an experience that I had with a client regarding checking the mail. He built a successful multi-million-dollar electrical company from the ground up that he has been running for nearly 30 years. When we were working to help him define his role and tasks in the company and identify the gap between what he was doing and what he wanted to be doing, the topic of checking the mail came up. He put on his list that he checked the mail every day. I immediately challenged that. Why would he be checking the mail when he paid several other administrative personnel that were more than capable of taking on that elementary task. His response was simple and quick, "because I enjoy doing it." After a little more probing, I learned that he wasn't dealing with the mail. He was simply pulling it from the mailbox, looking for any customer checks that might have been included in that day's stack, and handing the pile over to the girl at the front desk to process.

Even after running this business for so long, he enjoyed checking the mail because it made him feel good when checks written to his company arrived. "Well then," I said, "by all means, if you enjoy checking the mail, then don't stop!" The point of being a business owner is to love what you do and if a task like checking the mail is something you like to do, then do it.

Part of staying in your lane as married business partners—or any business partners for that matter, is knowing and understanding your unique abilities and those of your partner as well. Usually we know our own unique ability, but it can still be fun to do exercises like the DISC test or the Enneagram scale. If you are not familiar with either of these, the world wide web is full of resources on the subject. They can be just as fun as they are revealing of our personalities, tendencies and characteristics.

Do the best that you can to set you and your spouse up in a way that you both can spend the majority of your time within your unique abilities. In general, we don't like to do things that we aren't good at. I never really understood why so much of society suggests putting tons of effort into improving weaknesses. To me it's equivalent to suggesting a professional football player spend time improving his curve ball. Why spend time and effort improving something that is so far outside of his unique ability when he could be spending time perfecting something he's already reasonably good at? Leave the curve ball to the pitchers and work on perfecting that 2-point conversion. In the case of business, practice perfection on your strengths, and surround yourself with people whose strengths are your weaknesses. And don't forget, there is always outsourcing. If it makes reasonable sense to outsource, then do it. Think of the time and mental capacity you could free up by doing so.

When Justin and I worked through documenting our roles during coaching, the topic of who should do sales came up. Justin put sales on his list of what he thought he should be doing. At that time our business was large enough that we really could have created an entire sales department, or at least had one person dedicated to sales nearly full-time, yet Justin still had sales under his roles. Christina saw this and immediately began to question his reasoning.

"Justin, why do you have sales on your list when your company is clearly of the size that you should have someone else closing deals?" Christina asked.

"Because I am really good at sales," Justin said matter-of-factly.

Christina and Justin are two relatively strong people, so I sat back and listened quietly, wondering how this conversation was going to unfold.

Christina continued the questioning. "But as the business owner and entrepreneur, you are supposed to be doing higher level, strategic things like driving the business towards its vision. How can you expect to do that if you are also the sales guy?"

I could see Justin's eyebrows harden and could hear the irritation in his voice. There's no doubt Christina could feel the tension building, but she did not back down.

"Because not only am I good at sales, but I enjoy it," he rebutted.

"Do you *really* enjoy sales, or are you afraid that no one else can do it as well as you can?" she prodded. My mouth fell open a little. Did she really just say that? Oh man, I thought, this isn't going to end well.

"Yes," he said confidently, "I really do enjoy sales. There is so much of this leadership and entrepreneurial stuff that is hard, and sales is something that comes naturally to me. I thoroughly enjoy it, and I don't want to give up the part of business that I enjoy to potentially fill it with more things I don't enjoy."

"Ok, that's fair," Christina said, satisfied that she had gotten to the real reason why he had sales on his list of roles. I felt myself exhale and realized I had been holding my breath for the duration of that conversation. It's not often that anyone challenges Justin, but Christina did so gracefully while getting to the reason under the reason. Just like why I questioned my client about checking the mail, she was questioning Justin about sales to make sure the reason he did it was legit.

Once you and your business partner become clear on your individual roles the next part, and potentially the hardest part, is sticking to your own roles. As tempting as it may be, you do you and let your partner do them. If you have questions about how your partner is performing his or her tasks, ask out of love and genuine curiosity. Avoid judgement and don't assume they are wrong; if anything, assume you are wrong and seek understanding and clarity from your partner. On the same note, do what you say you are going to do. Fulfill your roles to the best of your ability and if your spouse asks for clarity, give it without getting defensive.

CHAPTER 5

Communication

"Seek first to understand and then to be understood." —Dr. Steven Covey

We have talked to many married couples who are also business partners, and there is one opportunity for growth and improvement that seems common among them all—communication. According to www.businessdictionary.com, the definition of communication is "Two-way process of reaching mutual understanding, in which participants not only exchange (encode-decode) information, news, ideas and feelings but also create and share meaning. In general, communication is a means of connecting people or places. In business, it is a key function of management--an organization cannot operate without communication between levels, departments and employees."

Human beings are blessed with the most sophisticated ability to communicate compared to all other living species, and yet we still struggle with fine tuning the skill. Even though human communication is multi-dimensional - verbal, non-verbal, written—there are often misunderstandings or miscommunications. Signals get crossed, words are said… or left unsaid; tone is misperceived, and communication breakdowns occur.

Justin and I are not perfect at communicating with each other. We have certainly dealt with the frustrations that come along with communication breakdowns. Over the years we have spent a lot of time and a lot of energy continually improving the way in which we communicate with each other. Like Dr. Steven Covey's quote says, "First seek to understand and then to be understood." We spent a lot of time trying to figure out how the other wanted to receive information. In the last chapter we briefly mentioned personality tests. These kinds of tests can be used as tools for communication. We all hear and perceive things differently. We all interpret words, tone and body language in a different way, and that's part of what makes us unique as humans. Knowing and understanding how your partner prefers to communicate can be extremely useful. Those personality tests are not only good for you to know yourself better but for you to know and understand those closest to you better.

As the visionary, Justin has always been full of ideas and opinions on things that can be done to generate revenue. What I did not understand early in our entrepreneurial adventure was that he didn't necessarily want to act on each and every idea that came from his mouth. He was expressing new ideas and course changes on a regular basis, and I felt like every time a new idea was spoken, it meant that we were for sure going that way…leading to constant uncertainty, risk, cash investment and change. And to be honest, more times than necessary he did end up going down the rabbit hole before we got clear on our vision. (For a more in depth look at vision, refer to Chapter 2.)

There was one business idea he had that resulted in quite an argument between us. We were both working full time in our plumbing company office in Florida, and we were about a year into coaching with Christina. Justin and I, with Christina's guidance, were developing the structure of our appliance business in Atlanta and the plumbing business in Florida. We were finally starting to get some relief from the constant overwhelm that we had been experiencing for years prior. There were a couple of managers in place, many of our policies were written and being implemented, but there were still a couple of tasks we were doing that should have been delegated to employees. The businesses were finally starting to release the choke hold on our mental and emotional welfare.

Justin was working in his office, and I walked in and sat down at the chair in front of his desk. Shortly before, he had emailed me a set of financial statements and an asset list of a company asking if I would review them and let him know what I thought. I was irritated by the email because I didn't understand why he wanted me to look at these financials; after all, I was busy with the tasks from the two existing businesses. Because I was already irritated, I sat there in front of him, slumped in my chair, with too little patience for the conversation that was about to ensue.

"Did you look at those financial statements I emailed you?" he asked.

"I glanced at them," I said shortly.

"Well, what did you think?" he said.

"I don't know, why?" I said.

"That business is for sale. I looked at the financial statements and the asset list, and I think we should buy it," he said excitedly. "It's an existing business here in the area, and I think we could put a small amount of time and effort into it, and it could be incredibly profitable."

"Seriously?" I asked, almost sarcastically. "Are you seriously considering purchasing a business right now? We already have two businesses, one of which struggles to break even every month and we still have quite a bit to do on both. I definitely don't have the time or mental bandwidth to take on another business right now."

"Yeah, but the business is only $130k, and the assets themselves are worth more than that. Not to mention the fact that it's been profitable for the last three years, and the profit margin is pretty incredible. It really wouldn't take that much of our time—it seems like a no brainer to me," he said.

I stopped listening. He was presenting his case as to why this was a good idea and it was sounding like so many other ideas he had before that were never acted upon. I figured this would soon blow over and then, maybe he could get back to work on the two businesses that were already taking all our attention and effort. I made a mistake this time though. This time I verbalized exactly what I was thinking. Usually there's a filter between what I think and what I say, but this time the filter had likely been pulled by whatever ridiculousness I was dealing with that day prior to this conversation.

I sighed. "Here's the deal," I said. "I get you are excited about this opportunity." I air-quoted the last word. "But I am not really going to put a lot of thought or effort into whether this business is a good investment because like so many of your ideas, it'll blow over and I'll have wasted time thinking about it. You have a lot of ideas that don't ever come to reality, and this is likely another one of those."

His face immediately changed from enthusiasm to angry. "No," he said curtly. "This is something I really want to do, and I am sharing it with you because you are my wife and my business partner. But don't worry about it. I won't share any of my ideas with you anymore. Sorry to have interrupted your day."

"Come on," I said defensively. "I didn't mean to piss you off. But you have to admit that you have lots of ideas that never go anywhere. I get that you think purchasing this business is a good idea, but I don't think it is. I don't think we can spare the time or money into taking on another business right now."

"Don't worry about it. Forget I even brought it up," he said defiantly. I knew the conversation was over, and he had shut down. I was mad, he was mad, and there was no point continuing. I got up from the chair in front of his desk, went back to my office, shut my door and fumed about the conversation that had just taken place.

The emotion of that discussion quickly blew over, and life went on as usual for a couple of days. We eventually talked about that business again which was a sign to me that he really was serious about this particular idea. Usually the idea isn't going to stick, and I only hear about it once, but the fact that he brought it up again, told me I should start considering this business as a possible investment.

We ended up purchasing the business, and it is now part of our entrepreneurial portfolio. We have since discussed that conversation and now laugh when we think of what we learned about each other as a result. I learned that I should continue to listen to Justin's ideas, participate in those conversations when they come up but not to really put a lot of thought into the particular idea until it comes up a second or third time. Justin learned that it's better to filter some of his ideas before he tells me about them. He has learned that I am not a huge fan of change unless it's my idea so when he has an idea, he is really serious about, he warms me up to the idea before just blurting out his plan.

Justin jumps in: And can we add that not only did we end up purchasing the business, but it is also successful and takes very little of our time? So yes, I was right on this one—but I will admit, there were other things in which we invested in the past that didn't pan out the same way so I can certainly see her skepticism.

This example of the way in which Justin and I chose to communicate with each other put a spotlight on how important it is to understand the way in which a spouse and business partner receives communication. Because we are two different people with two different social skills and preferences, it only makes sense that we give and receive information differently. This is so for anyone you communicate with. Not everyone wants to receive information the way you do and accommodating their communication style, especially on a very important or sensitive subject can many times make facilitating the conversation easier or more effective.

JUSTIN

Kristen and I worked with a medium-size home services company in Connecticut. The owners, a married couple, had spent the last eight years building a company and had managed to achieve $8.5M in annual sales. With those sales, they were managing nearly a million dollars of cash flow in and out of their business each month. Their management structure was similar to many other businesses we have worked with. He managed the operations and his wife managed the money. We had seen small examples of their lack of communication show up in their business already, but this particular instance was a huge breakdown.

About six months into coaching with them, the client shared with me that they were right in the middle of a serious cash crisis.

"Well, Justin," he said that day on our call. "I got some shocking and unexpected news from my wife yesterday."

"Ok," I said, pausing to let him continue.

The client took a deep breath and let it out with a long sigh. "My wife shared with me that the business is out of cash," he began.

"What do you mean by out of cash?" I asked sympathetically.

"Like completely out of cash," he said. "But that's not all."

"Ok," I said again giving the space for him to continue.

"Apparently we haven't received a paycheck from the business in almost a year."

Under normal circumstances, this particular client has an extremely calm disposition so when he spoke about their cash flow crisis with me, he wasn't angry, and his words were not heated. Instead he spoke quietly, slowly, almost calculated—like a man who was processing feelings of guilt and embarrassment simultaneously.

He said aloud what I was thinking and what he had likely asked himself a hundred times in the last 20 hours.

"How did I not see this coming?" he asked. "How did I not know I haven't been paid in almost a year? Why in the world didn't she come to me with this so I could help solve it before it turned into a full-blown crisis?"

At that moment there wasn't much I could say or do to make the situation any better. This situation that had blown up in his hands manifested from the lack of communication between him and his wife. It wasn't even a *mis*communication, or a communication *breakdown*; it was completely non-existent communication which led to a major problem within their business and their marriage. This lack of communication affected everyone they employed and their families, nearly 100 people. Their business was now operating in crisis mode; they were scrambling to collect on receivables, cutting employees' hours and talking with the bank about opening a line of credit.

After the client was able to put a tourniquet on the cash flow situation and stop the bleeding for the short term, we dug in during the following coaching calls to find and solve the root of the lack of communication between he and his wife regarding their current cash situation. We discovered that she didn't want to be the one that caused her husband any more stress than he was already under. She saw the issue coming for quite some time but thought she could handle the situation and correct it herself, so she didn't say anything to him. The problem was, she waited entirely too long before she spoke up and what started out as a small cash flow problem that could have been solved with a few minor tweaks early on…now, snowballed into an avalanche of a problem that nearly took them out of business.

We created and implemented a communication tool for them to use and share between them on a weekly basis. It's called a Cash on Hand Report, and it shows the current cash balances of each bank account as well as the current amount due to credit card companies and any primary vendors they use that carry large balances. It is compiled in an Excel spreadsheet, and it looks something like this:

Cash on Hand Report
as of:
(current date)

Bank Account 1	Current Balance
Bank Account 2	Current Balance
Bank Account 3	Current Balance
Total	**$0.00**

PYMNT DUE DATE			Points/Miles/Cash Back Rewards	
Sept 5	Credit Card #1	Current Balance	xxx,xxx	Points
Sept 8	Credit Card #2	Current Balance	$xxx.xx	Cash Reward Balance
Sept 12	Major Vendor #1	Current Balance		
Sept 25	Major Vendor #2	Current Balance		
	Total	**$0.00**		

We set up a schedule so that on the same day each week she would fill out this report and send it to him so he would be aware of the current bank balances as well as what was due to the major credit cards and vendors. While this report does not show all money that is due to all vendors, it at least captures the one with the highest balances. Knowing that he is the visionary and doesn't want to be bothered by tons of details, we decided to curate the information to give him enough to be informed but not enough that he would be bogged down with too many details. Allowing her to present him with this information weekly also took the pressure off her to decide at what point it was appropriate to include him when an issue arose. He could now see the weekly cash situation, and he too could see if an issue was coming. This report relieved her of the feeling of having to be the bearer of bad news and removed the emotion from the information. Assuming the report was used as intended, never again would he be surprised by a cash flow crisis, and she felt like he was informed enough to help solve any future cash flow crunches before they turned into a crisis.

This particular report also solves a problem that we've seen before, especially when the husband is the spender and the wife is the saver or vice versa. If the wife is in charge of the financial side of the business, she is usually aware of large bills coming down the pipeline that the husband may not be aware of. A lot of the time, these large bills include payroll taxes, income taxes or business insurance premiums. It is easy for these types of bills to be overlooked by the husband-technician-spenders because they are not even on their radar to be aware. They don't see the bills come in, nor should they, and since often these bills are paid less often than monthly, the wife anticipates them coming and the husband doesn't.

These larger, non-monthly bills can and should be included on the Cash on Hand Report, so the husband-technician-spender can also be aware of them. Perhaps there is a piece of equipment or a large tool he would like to purchase. If he sees a comfortable amount of cash in the bank and isn't aware of a payroll tax bill the wife is preparing, he might purchase the equipment without consulting her (communication breakdown) and the money she anticipated paying the tax bill with is now spent.

On the other end of the communication spectrum is exaggeration. Not only can *not* communicating cause problems, so can using language that describes a situation or issue as much larger than it really is. There are certain words in the English language that signify totality. The most common are *always*, *never* and *every*. These are very strong words and if we were to be very honest, rarely are these words used in the right context. Perhaps we use the word *always* when in reality *sometimes* is more appropriate.

I met a business owner a couple years ago and the more I talked with her, the more I noticed that she used words of totality very often; notice I didn't say always. She'd say things like, "Every time I go to the bank, it takes like 30 minutes to get through the teller line."

However, in reality, it only takes three to five minutes except last time it took longer because she was there on a busy Friday afternoon on a day the bank was shorthanded.

Or she'd say, "My employees never follow the system I have created for answering the phone," when really what happens is they are answering it correctly most of the time. She just happened to walk by the other day and heard part of a conversation that she didn't like.

The unfortunate part about her overusing words of totality is that once the people she was communicating with realized that she didn't really mean *always, never* and *every,* they began to tune out or not take her seriously when she spoke because they assumed she was exaggerating the situation. It reminds me of a children's fable, "The Boy That Cried Wolf." In the rare instance that an issue she might describe is not exaggerated, she can't get any traction from her employees to get it resolved because they can't tell what is real and what isn't.

As business owners, we often *feel like* a situation is different, better or worse, than it actually is. The best way to match a feeling with reality is to quantify. For example, if you *feel like* the phone isn't getting answered right, then you take some time to observe each time it is answered and track the results with actual numbers. If the phone is answered 100 times that day you tally and of those 100 times, five are answered incorrectly, then it becomes very clear that the perceived problem is actually smaller than originally presumed.

Quantification goes the other way, too. Maybe I *feel like* an issue is small and not a big deal. But what if I track the issue and realize after I put numbers to it, the effect is far more compounded then I originally thought? This actually happened to me in the accounting department, specifically collections. I didn't feel like it was that big of a deal if a customer paid us at 45 days instead of at 30 days when the bill was actually due. I didn't push the issue; we got paid when we got paid and usually didn't charge late fees if it was only a little late.

Then I was presented with an interesting perspective. When we are not paid quickly and not charging interest or late fees, we are essentially loaning money to customers interest free. Same as cash. If that customer were to go anywhere else to get the money to pay us sooner, they would have to pay interest or fees to borrow the money. So why are we allowing them to borrow the money from us interest free? On top of that, what could we be doing with that cash if the invoice sat in accounts receivable for half the time it sits there now? And one step farther, how much administrative time could be saved, i.e., payroll dollars, if we didn't wait so long to start collections because we all know the older the invoice, the harder it is to collect.

Once I took a little bit of time to put actual hard numbers to our accounts receivable turnover, I realized how important it was to get those bills collected sooner and therefore made some systems shifts to make it happen.

As the relationship with my client developed, I was intrigued by the reasoning behind why she felt the need to use words of totality to get her point across. Occasionally I would gently challenge her bold statements and many times just repeating back exactly what she said was enough to make her stop and reconsider whether the problem or frustration was really happening "always," "never" or "every" time. Until I pointed out what she was doing and how she was communicating, she didn't see that the words she was choosing were an issue. After all, she wasn't being untruthful or lying, she truly believed she was accurately describing the situation.

With her permission during one of our coaching sessions, we pulled back the curtain on what was causing her to automatically and usually unnecessarily make the jump to words of totality. I took her through a disassociation exercise in which she observed in her mind's eye a conversation she recently had with her husband and who was also her business partner. She had shared with me before the exercise that she wanted to take over a couple new tasks within the business because she felt she could make a more efficient system and ultimately create a new way to save the company money. When she made this suggestion to her husband though, he immediately shut her down telling her that the problems she thought she saw weren't large enough to do anything about at the moment. She left the conversation feeling unheard and that her ideas and opinions were unimportant.

"I invite you to do a mental exercise with me," I suggested during that coaching session.

"Ok," she said hesitantly.

"Awesome," I smiled. "Don't worry, it's not something you can do right or wrong. Its purpose is to highlight perspective and mindset. Cool?"

"Cool," she affirmed.

"Excellent," I began. "Start by getting comfortable in your chair. Take a deep breath in and on your exhale blow out loud enough for me hear through the phone."

I took a deep breath with her in…and blew the air out with an audible deflation of my lungs.

"Next," I said, "continue to take quiet, deep breaths in and out, allowing your shoulders to relax and when you are ready, close your eyes."

I gave her a few seconds to settle in and release any tension she was holding.

"Now," I said, "in your mind's eye, we are going to walk through that conversation between you and your husband again, but this time I want you to watch it happening as if you were watching two strangers having a conversation. You are not looking at him. You are looking at the both of you, as if you were watching the conversation take place on a television."

"Evaluate the scene you are watching in your mind's eye. What is the feeling of the room? Look at the body language; what does it tell you? Is he giving her his full attention? Is she giving him her full attention? Listen to the descriptive words that are being used. How many times did you hear words like 'always,' 'never' and 'every' during the conversation between these two people on the TV?"

"Good, ok now take the TV remote in your hand and press the channel up button. You have changed the channel to another conversation you had between you and your husband where you didn't feel heard. Again, you are watching the conversation as if it's on TV and between two strangers."

"Evaluate this new scene you are watching in your mind's eye. What is the feeling of the room? Look at the body language, what does it tell you? Is he giving her his full attention? Is she giving him her full attention? Listen to the descriptive words that are being used and pay attention to when and how words like 'always,' 'never' and 'every' are used."

"Excellent. Now, replay the conversations, but this time I want you to turn up the volume on any sentence that starts with 'always,' 'never' or 'every.' What is being said? What point is trying to be heard? Should the sentence really and truly begin with 'always,' 'never' or 'every?' Does whoever is saying it really mean to express 100%?"

After a quiet moment she took a deep breath in, "No," she said. "I guess I don't mean every single time, but I really feel like what I am saying is important, and I need him to understand that."

"Ok," I said. "Open your eyes. What you are saying is very important. What do you think happens to his attentiveness when he hears an 'always,' 'never' or 'every' that isn't really always, never or every?"

"I don't know," she paused and looked down at her hands in her lap. "I guess maybe he doesn't believe me. Oh God, do I sound like the boy who cried wolf?"

"Well," I said. "How could the women on the TV screen have presented her suggestions to him more effectively?"

"I don't know, maybe not use 'always,' 'never' or 'every?'"

"Yes, that's one way," I said. "Another way is to state what you are feeling and end it with a question. You could say 'I feel like no one ever follows this policy. What do you think?'"

This allows you to express what you are feeling but also gives him the opportunity to start a discussion on the topic. Perhaps there is information you don't have about the topic. Or maybe what you saw or experienced just happened to be a once in ten problem. By asking questions, it allows you to get the information to fill in the blanks without having to make assumptions."

"I have some homework for you," I said. "Be aware of when you are about to use 'always,' 'never' or 'every' and ask yourself—*do I mean 100%?*"

We wrapped up our conversation that day, and a few weeks later I asked her about this topic we discussed. She was more aware of how often she used words of totality and was working to replace those words with more reasonable alternatives and was asking more questions to see if there was any information she was missing. She also reported that by doing this she and her husband have had some really good conversations about the ideas she has for the business.

The following questions are designed for internal reflection on your communication style versus your spouse and business partner's style. We recommend that you contemplate these questions individually first and them come together to discuss the results with each other.

GIVING

1. Think about a time you didn't feel heard.
2. What specific action or response made you feel that way?
3. List the emotions you processed during this particular interaction.
4. Why do you think you felt that way?
5. Consider who you were talking to when you didn't feel heard. What could you have done differently during the conversation, or how could you have presented the information differently to get a more desirable response? For example, could you have gotten to your point faster, or could you have provided more detail or background? Would there have been a better time of the day, day of the

week or, dare I say, time of the month to have the conversation?

6. Have you ever intentionally left out details to avoid confrontation or in hopes of getting your desired response?

RECEIVING

7. Has there ever been a time you didn't have all the info you needed to make a decision because of a lack of or breakdown of communication? What questions could you ask next time you think that is happening to feel confident you have all the important information?

8. At what stress level can you receive information and when can't you? (Picture the green card/red card like at a Brazilian steak house. Green means "yes, I am ready for more food" and Red means, "I am full and can't take any more.")

9. Do you give the person who is talking to you your full attention? Do you try to multi-task or does your mind wander when they are talking? If you answered, "Yes," to either or both of these, is it possible you could be missing some important cues either in tone or body language by multi-tasking?

Thank you for taking the time to thoughtfully and honestly think about and answer these questions and then discussing them with your spouse and business partner. This entire book and all its exercises are designed to be used as tools of communication, and it is our hope that through the exercises, we are able to help you facilitate open and productive conversations between the two of you.

The way business owners communicate with one another sets the tone for the culture among employees within the business. The level of respect, compassion and professionalism or lack thereof, exhibited to each other as owners is mirrored by the employees.

One example of how communication among owners can affect the employee culture can be seen in the reality TV show, *Orange County Choppers*. One of my first thoughts after watching that show for the first time was about how awful it would be to work there. The owners were constantly yelling at each other, throwing things and cussing. The show portrayed a tension in their workplace so thick you could cut it with a knife. I know the producers of the show were highlighting this behavior to entertain its viewers; however, the behavior portrayed in the show is not uncommon within small businesses especially when family is involved in the day to day operations.

If there is animosity between owners or if one owner has a shorter temper or less patience than the other, you will find that the employees will avoid the owner with a short fuse. After all, no one wants to be the one to set off that explosion. Both of you as owners need to have a united front. If there are any chinks in the armor, employees will find them. They will figure out which one of you they will receive the answer they want and go to that person with the question.

This came up in our business a couple of times. One example is related to cash advances on pay checks. Occasionally an employee would need some cash from their check prior to payday. Any time an employee asked me for a cash advance, I would tell them, "No." I was hard-hearted when it came to cash advances for employees.

I felt that it wasn't our problem if the employee couldn't manage finances well enough, and we were not a bank, so when an employee came to me with a cash issue, my response would be, "No, unfortunately we can't help, but here are a couple other options you may consider."

And then I would suggest options like asking a family member for help, getting a short-term loan from the bank or sell something. I know it sounds harsh, but I was afraid that if I said, "Yes," it would enable the poor money management by the employees.

Justin, on the other hand, was a different story. Nearly every time an employee asked him for a cash advance he would say, "Yes." They would usually tell him all about how they were struggling and if they didn't get the cash they needed, they wouldn't have enough money to put gas in their vehicle to get to work. Justin would feel like he was put in a bad spot because he needed the employees to be at work, and he worked so closely with them that in a way he felt responsible for their financial hardships.

It didn't take long for our employees to know which one of us to go to when they needed help before pay day. They stopped asking me because they knew I would deny the request, and every time they would go to Justin because they knew he would likely say, "Yes."

It took a couple of years and many cash advances granted, but eventually Justin changed his viewpoint on the concept.

He realized that when we let an employee have money before payday that the pay back was a challenge to manage—if we even got paid back at all. (We've had employees get a cash advance and then never show back up to work!) And he also started to see trends among employees when a cash advance was granted. It would create a vicious cycle and in the long run would enable the employees to continue to make poor financial decisions.

Now, we don't allow cash advances at all; once the employees realized both of us were on the same front, neither would grant a cash advance, they stopped asking. However, even though we don't allow cash advances anymore, we started offering to pay for them to attend Dave Ramsey's Financial Peace University with the goal of giving them the opportunity to move away from poor financial management and away from living paycheck to paycheck. (*You can find out more information at* <u>*www.financialpeaceuniversity.com*</u>.)

What is important here is being mindful of how you communicate with your spouse, not only when employees are around but also when it's just the two of you. Recognizing each other's strengths and weaknesses, knowing and under-standing each other's communication styles, presenting a united front for employees and respecting each other as busi-ness partner and spouse has the power to positively influence your entire team.

A couple of final thoughts on communication. In the business world a lot of thoughts and ideas are communicated through the written word. Emails, company memos, policies, instant messages, even text messages are exchanged between employees and employers on a regular basis. While these forms of communication are convenient, sometimes part of the message is left behind, or assumptions are made by the reader that were not intended by the author. As a matter of fact, I am certain there are even parts of this book that you read in a different context than what we are trying to portray. As an employer, business partner and spouse, it is important to know when a verbal, face to face conversation is appropriate.

An open and honest line of communication between you and your spouse is vital to the survival of your business and your marriage. For those of us that are *fixers*, it is very tempting to try to solve problems the other might be expressing. We love our partner, and we don't want them to be hurting or struggling, so our gut reaction is to swoop in and solve the problem. Sometimes that is exactly what is needed.

And sometimes the other person just needs to be heard.

CHAPTER 6

Your Social Circle

"People come into your life for a reason, a season or a lifetime." —author unknown

"If you hang out with chickens, you are going to cluck. If you hang out with eagles, you are going to fly." —Dr. Steve Maraboli

KRISTEN

I recently met a client for dinner. She and her husband had just bought into a local HVAC company, and for the first time in their lives were now in the business owner role. I could see the moment I sat down in front of her at that small restaurant during the dinner rush that all was not well. She looked exhausted, her eyes were puffy as if she'd recently been crying, her hair normally fashionably styled was now pinned in an unkept bun on the top of her head. I could immediately tell by her expression that even though she had only been a business owner for a couple short months, she was already drowning in complete overwhelm.

We exchanged pleasantries and talked about the upcoming employee appreciation event they were planning and the community activities they would participate in that weekend. After the waitress put our drinks down in front of us, I asked how she was *really* doing in her new role as business owner.

When the simple question of how are you doing rolled off my tongue, tears began to well in her eyes as she desperately tried to keep her composure and answer the question as we sat at the small booth in a restaurant surrounded by strangers.

"This is way more difficult than I thought it would be," she said.

"Ok," I responded. "In what way?"

"I am trying to process all these changes, and I feel like there is no one I can speak honestly with. I don't want to share my stressors with my husband because I already know he's just as overwhelmed as I am," she said. "And, no one in my family understands where I am coming from. None of them own businesses and honestly, I think most of them feel I have no room to voice frustrations because we brought this on ourselves."

"I can understand and relate to those feelings," I told her.

She continued, "And what I really never saw coming is how buying this business would drive a wedge between my friends and me. Here's the deal, I can handle no one in my family relating to what we have going on, and I'm ok with that, but even though I am never alone, I feel unbelievably isolated."

Interested in allowing her to vent all of her frustrations I said, "Tell me more."

"Well," she said. "That's where the issue lies. My friends are employees of the company we bought. That didn't matter before we were owners, but now that we have assumed that role, the dynamic has changed. I can't tell them my frustrations about the business because they are now my employees—and many times they *are* the frustrations!"

She continued, "And even if they aren't, the frustration is that I can't share with them my fears and anxieties about running the business because I am now supposed to be their fearless leader."

I sat quietly and simply listened. I got the feeling that she didn't really want solutions to her problems, she just needed the opportunity in which to release some of the thoughts she had been holding in. You see, her social circle consisted of employees and employees' wives of the company they had just purchased. Prior to their purchase, those friendships were all on the same level, that of peers. The synergy of those relationships was turned on its ear after the purchase though. No longer could she use those friends as a sounding board because they either wouldn't understand or couldn't know the sensitive business information that she needed to express out loud to another human being.

"I feel like I am surrounded by people that I have to now keep at an arm's length distance. I never anticipated the feeling of isolation among all the people I am surrounded by on a daily basis," she confided.

"And to top it off, I am beginning to realize," she continued, "that the people who are taking the brunt of my overwhelm and frustration are my kids. I notice I don't have the patience I once had with them, and I find myself snapping at them a lot more often then I used to."

She was trying to internally process being a business owner with nowhere to express herself. Even though starting a business from the ground up and entering an established business are two very different experiences, I still very much understood the positive and negative effects being a business owner can have on what was previously known as a social life. I also understood and could relate to being married to a man that was always striving for more and better. I could completely relate to what she was saying and feeling—I had gone through that same evolution years before and I could feel my body mirroring her emotion as she gushed all the things she has been holding back from her husband and her friends-turned-employees.

Within the first year or two after Justin and I started our business, I came to the realization that our social life was changing dramatically. The group of friends that we spent the majority of our spare time with were slowly disconnecting from us and us from them. The deeper we got in our business, the less we had in common with them and quite frankly, the less time we had to properly nurture those relationships. They all worked for other people which meant in most cases they were able to turn their brain off work when they weren't there, and they certainly weren't thinking about how their employer was going to handle the cashflow or designing new marketing material or staying in compliance with the IRS and local jurisdictions. They just had to show up, do their job and go home. None of them had to think about any of that nor did they express the desire to do anything different. We no longer had very much spare time and had to say, "No," to the majority of the social invitations they extended to us because we were working in our business. Before long, our place in the group was filled with new friends and the invitations stopped coming. There was no event or fallout that marked the end of the relationships with the particular circle of friends; we just all grew apart.

I struggled with the same feelings of isolation during the early years in our business. I too kept a lot from my family because I assumed they wouldn't understand or be able to relate. As you likely already know, owning a business isn't always roses, sunshine and monetary success. I didn't want to share the ugly times in our business with my family because I didn't want them to think we were failures or irresponsible or careless or any of the other negative adjectives that were associated with my irrational fears. Above all else, I wanted them to be proud of us and in my head if I shared my fears, frustrations, and overwhelm with them when our business was in its infancy, then I ran the risk of them thinking otherwise of me.

I had a hard time making new friends—partially because I didn't have a whole lot of time to spend developing meaningful relationships and partially because there weren't a lot of business owners that were as young as we were at the time. (Also, I am an introvert, so there's that. I can laugh at that now, but at the time I hated that making friends and letting people in were so difficult.) Many business owners we met were much older than we were, and their businesses were more mature, so I felt a disconnect there, too. Although, now that I think about it, those business owners would have probably been great connection points had I been willing to become vulnerable and ask for help.

One day, after a couple years of cordial and surface level relationships that mainly developed out of convenience, I came to a realization that completely changed my mindset around that feeling of isolation. It was a late November day in North Georgia, and I was lost in thought standing in our master bathroom staring out the picture window behind the bathtub. The sky was cloudy and the dormant grass in the backyard turned brown from the cool weather making the view relatively drab. Even though I was staring out the window, I wasn't really looking at the view; I was thinking about this concept of friendships versus isolation. All of a sudden, a thought popped into my head. From whatever the source, God, The Universe or some other thing which was greater than me came, "It's ok."

Immediately a sense of peace warmed my body on that chilly, sunless day. It was almost like I was given permission to move on from those that I needed to move on from to make room for those I hadn't yet met.

"It's ok," I thought. "I don't have to stress about the ebb and flow of friendships because it's all ok."

I shared this new mindset with the young woman sitting across the table who I could see was hoping I would share with her a simple solution to make it all better.

I told her about that moment when I realized that we as humans spend our lives in periods of growth and just like we physically outgrow our things as children, we mentally and emotionally outgrow relationships throughout our lives as well. Think about it I told her, you are likely not friends with the same people you were friends with during elementary school, or middle school or as teenagers. Sure, there might be a couple people from your childhood that you connect with periodically to swap parenting stories, but those relationships likely lack the depth needed to feel heard and understood from the unique perspective of business owner.

I shared with her that I spent much of the time prior to my mindset shift mourning the loss of these friendships until I understood that it's ok. It's ok to grow personally and professionally. It's ok to thoroughly enjoy a friendship while it positively influences your life, and it's equally ok to let the relationship go when it no longer lifts you up.

Jim Rohn, entrepreneur and author, made a wonderful point when he said, "We are the average of the five people we spend the most time with."

If you strive to improve yourself and your business, you must surround yourself with people that are better than you so you can be stretched, encouraged and motivated to grow personally and professionally.

I could tell by her tense eyebrows and wrinkled forehead that what I was sharing with her wasn't what she wanted to hear.

"Nope," she said. "I simply can't imagine not being friends in the future with who I am friends with now."

"And maybe you *will* be friends with them forever," I said. "But perhaps, you won't."

I think she was hoping I'd tell her a way that she could bridge the divide that was growing between her and her current social circle and did not hesitate to express her disbelief that maybe it couldn't be done. In that moment she just could not imagine that those that she spent most of her spare time with now likely wouldn't be those that she spent that time with in the future.

I didn't debate or argue in an attempt to prove my point, but I knew that deep down in her she now had subconscious permission to begin to let go and move away from relationships that no longer lifted her up.

JUSTIN

The concept that we are the average of the five people that we spend the most time with has been one of a handful of important mantras in our house for many years. It is something that we openly discuss with our children as they grow older and begin to choose the circle of friends they run with. When our children are young, we are able to control who they hang out with but as they begin to mature, our reach into their social lives shortens.

As adults we see countless stories of teenagers that are good kids but become wrapped up with the wrong crowd. They are peer pressured into doing things that they normally wouldn't do mainly because they choose to surround themselves with friends that pull them down instead of lift them up. The younger a teenager can truly understand this concept the better—which is why we started talking about this topic with our children long before their teenage years. We figured we'd talk about it while they still listened to us because as many parents have experienced...once children become teenagers, they suddenly know much more than you and as the parent, you no longer know what you are talking about.

Research has proven that the people that are closest to us influence the way we think, the way we feel, and ultimately our level of success. Moran Cerf, a neuroscientist at Northwestern University has studied this topic extensively for years. He said, "The more we study engagement, we see time and again that just being next to certain people actually aligns your brain with them based on their mannerisms, the smell of the room, the noise level, and many other factors. This means the people you hang out with actually have an impact on your engagement with reality beyond what you can explain. And one of the effects is you become alike."

King Solomon even talks about social circles in the Old Testament of the Bible. In Proverbs 13:20, he says, "Walk with the wise and become wise, for a companion of fools suffers harm."

I embraced this philosophy with open arms and immediately went in search of people and groups that were more successful than I. That's not to say I dropped my friends like hot potatoes, but I did begin to actively search for a few new connections that could provide the stretch that I wasn't necessarily getting from my current environment. I certainly don't follow the average of 5 people rule to the word, but it has made me become more aware of who I choose to spend my time with. As business owners, we all have limited time to spend with friends so why would we choose to fill that time hanging out with those that have low personal or professional aspirations? Remember back to our discussion in Chapter 3 about time management. Just like we have to be greedy with our time in our business, we have to do the same for our personal lives. We all only have 24 hours in a day, and the concept of saying, "Yes," to one thing means you are saying, "No," to something else applies here as well. Who are you saying, "Yes," to? And on the flip side, who are you saying, "No" to?

It's also worth mentioning that just because we choose to seek out those that are better than we are, every single interaction and conversation doesn't have to be of personal or professional improvement nature. There are times when stretch conversations are needed and appropriate, and there are times when simple casual conversations about normal life are the better choice. And, value can be found in conversations with friends that have different mindsets and beliefs than our own. The point here is to have awareness of your social circle, without having blinders to block out anyone who has chosen a different life trajectory.

Another thing to keep in mind about this people-average philosophy is that there's a pretty good chance that literally the five people you truly spend the most time with consist of your spouse, children, and key employees or managers in your business. It is unrealistic to think that it would be appropriate to disconnect from these people, but that doesn't mean you should turn a blind eye on how those relationships affect you and your growth.

KRISTEN

I think the most relatable example outside of the business world regarding the drifting in and out of social circles is parenthood. Having kids is life changing in literally every way possible.

If we have friends that become parents before us, we find less and less to talk about because all they talk about is their baby. There is less and less in common between the two and many times that's enough to cause friends to drift apart. The new parents tend to drift towards other new parents because they both now have something to talk to each other about for hours.

This parental drift happens again as the kids get older. We tend to lean towards parents with kids the same age; even parents of very young children can struggle to find commonalities with parents of teenagers.

At this juncture of writing, I am feeling the need to add a disclaimer. By no means am I suggesting that it's impossible or unhealthy to have lifetime friends. Nor am I saying that once you have kids, you can't be friends with your non-kid friends anymore. Give yourself some slack though. Remember a few chapters ago when I said that time is an unlimited resource? Well, is the time you are investing in your current social circle getting a great ROI?

I invite you to engage in an exercise. This may not be easy to complete, but it is our hope that it shines some light on whether the people you spend your free time with lift you up or pull you down. This is a time to be completely and truly 100% honest with yourself, and I would encourage you to answer these questions in a quiet and safe environment.

1.   List names of five people you spend the most time with, not including your children and identify at least three of their most dominant traits and characteristics.

Name	Traits
1	
2	
3	
4	
5	

2.   List names of people in your network that provide stretch; identify their traits and characteristics.

Name	Traits
1	
2	
3	
4	
5	

3.   List names of people whose relationship is difficult or requires a lot of work. Identify their traits and

characteristics and the topics that tend to dominate your conversations. At what point is it appropriate to identify a relationship as toxic?

Name	Traits	Dominating Topics
1		
2		
3		
4		
5		

4. List names of people you would want in your circle assuming you could choose anyone in the world. What traits or characteristics do they have that appeal to you?

Name	Traits
1	
2	
3	
4	
5	

5. List three most common traits identified in #3.

Traits
1
2
3

6. List three most common traits identified in #2 and #4.

Traits
1
2
3

7. How do the traits you identified in #1 line up with #6?

8. Is it time to look for and add people to your circle whose traits line up with #6?

This exercise should be completed by you and your spouse individually. It is equally as important for you as a couple to have some people in your social circle that are connected as it is for you to have people in your life that provide stretch individually. This gives you the opportunity to grow personally and professionally as a power couple as well as for you and your spouse to grow independently.

Like you will see in many of the exercises in this book, we encourage you to complete this exercise apart from each other and then come together and talk about it afterwards. This has the potential of facilitating an excellent conversation between the two of you, and it will certainly raise your awareness of how your social circle is affecting your personal and professional growth.

JUSTIN

Kristen and I were talking about the creation of this chapter and spent some time reflecting on the last several years in terms of those that have entered and gone and those that have entered and are still present. When we start really looking at the traits and characteristics of those that we spend the most time with now, we see many traits we have in common. Our circle of friends now are not only business owners, but they are also health conscious and very driven individuals. Of our friends that are married, most have been so for quite a long time. They are financially responsible, strive for success and all of them work hard and play hard. We have made a conscious effort to surround ourselves with people who stretch us, and we have also made a point to spend time with people who appreciate being stretched by us.

As humans we crave spending time with like-minded people who share the same values and visions. We want to be part of a tribe, a community; we are pack animals. That is precisely what we are creating within our mastermind group, and that sense of community is what gives us the motivation to continue to drive engagement among members. The members in our mastermind group learn from each other and are eager to help the other business owners in the group, and in some cases, they are competitors in the same market.

I worked with my childhood best friend (other than my wonderful wife) for several years. He was a friend before he was an employee and for a while, we were able to navigate the boundaries that outlined the personal friendship and the employment relationship. During our teenage years we had so much in common. We played the same sports, ran with the same group of friends and caused the same amount of havoc for our high school teachers. Even through our twenties, we still had a lot in common—got married, had kids, and enjoyed too many gallons of hops to mention together. He knew everything about me and me him.

I am very driven and always striving for more and this trait that I possess has the potential to drive a wedge between me and others in my life. Sadly, towards the end of our working relationship it became apparent that we had different drive and values. The misalignment caused us both to not understand why the other would do and say what he did.

During one of our conversations he said, "You forgot where you came from."

"No," I immediately rebutted. "I remember exactly where I came from, and I work my ass off every single day to continue to grow from there."

That conversation solidified for me that I am doing exactly what I should be doing, and I strive every day to get better to learn more and to grow personally and professionally. If self-improvement is your gig, you won't find yourself fitting into the masses of those that are content where they are. As Dr. Seuss says, "Why fit in when you were born to stand out?"

The quote mentioned on the opening page of this chapter puts a nice bow on this gift of social circles:

> *"People come into our lives for a reason, a season or a lifetime," says an unknown author.*

As with so many things in life, awareness is key. Maybe you have some social changes to make. Maybe you don't. But being aware of how you spend your social time and with whom could very well mean the difference between ordinary and extraordinary.

Choose wisely, love deeply and give yourself permission to grow when necessary.

CHAPTER 7

Boundaries

"Balance is not better time management, it's better boundary management." —Unknown

"A lack of boundaries invites a lack of respect." —An Iota of Truth

"Healthy boundaries are not walls. They are the gates and fences that allow you to enjoy the beauty of our own garden." —Lydia H. Hall, as shared with Peg Streep

"Stop asking why they keep doing it and start asking why you keep allowing it" —Word Porn

Examples of boundaries and boundary violations can be found in just about every chapter in this book. It is such an important topic that we wanted to draw it out and discuss it in detail. Boundaries can already be a struggle in normal workplace environments, and they can be compounded when the workplace includes family members.

During our years of research for this book, we have seen examples of how family relationships have gone really well in business, and we have seen how they have gone really wrong in business. We have even experienced both sides of the coin at some point or another in our own businesses and within our marriage.

Boundaries don't always have to do with relationships though. Boundaries can be applied to your relationship with yourself and your health or money, and it can also be applied to time and even communication and conversations.

We are going to shake it up a little bit in this chapter and do the exercise in the beginning. I'd like for you to take the following quiz on boundaries to see where you score on healthy boundaries. Later we'll go into detail on each question to examine the positive and negative effects of each one.

Read each question. Every time you can honestly say, "Yup, that's me," give yourself a point.

1. I am so busy I don't have time for anything else. I am constantly running around like a chicken with my head cut off, and if someone asks me to do one more thing, I'll go into meltdown mode.
2. I am not comfortable saying, "No," to requests from other people—I don't want to disappoint or inconvenience them.
3. I employ friends—hey, they need a job and I need an employee—sounds like a win/win! Besides, I trust my friend better than a stranger anyway.
4. I have a hard time treating friends that are employees the same way that I treat employees that are not friends.

5. I employ family members. After all, I love my brother. Why wouldn't I want to work with him?

6. I have a hard time treating family members that are employees the same way that I treat employees that are not family members. I can be harder on my brother because he's, well, my brother!

7. I don't have a clear definition between home life and business life; I often work on business tasks at home and deal with home life issues at the office.

8. My business almost always interferes with my family activities. I miss many of my kids' extra-curricular activities, and I couldn't tell you the last time I had a date night with my spouse.

9. When my spouse and I do go on a date, all we have to talk about is the business. If we vow not to talk about the business, then we sit in awkward silence listening to each other chew.

10. I don't have hobbies outside of my business. Hobbies?! Yeah, right—who has time for those??!!

7pts-10pts—I have absolutely no boundaries—any improvement would be great.

4pts-6pts—I have some boundaries but there is room for improvement in my life.

0pts-3pts—I have a pretty good handle on boundaries but as with anything, I can fine tune some areas.

These questions are designed to be extreme, and perhaps even coaxed out a chuckle from you. While they sound extreme, there is a pretty good chance you can (or could have in the past) relate to each and every question in one way or another. How did you score on this quiz? This is a good quiz to take every few months to evaluate your boundaries and whether you need to take action to set clear boundaries in any area.

Let's look at each quiz question a little more deeply.

1. I am so busy I don't have time for anything else. I am constantly running around like a chicken with my head cut off and if someone asks me to do one more thing, I'll go into complete meltdown mode.

If you can identify with this question, you are likely operating in overwhelm. It is extremely difficult to run a successful business and participate in a fulfilling marriage when you are operating in this manner. What are you doing that keeps you this busy? How do your time management skills and strategies, or lack thereof, fuel this particular fire? I would be willing to bet that if you related to this question, there is a good chance you could identify with the next question as well.

As we go through and talk about the rest of the questions, and as you work on implementing some of the strategies we speak about in this chapter, you will find that a side effect of implementation will be the ability to un-identify with this first question.

Let's look at the next question.

2. I am not comfortable saying, "No," to requests from other people—I don't want to disappoint or inconvenience them.

This question refers to time management which we discussed in great detail in Chapter 3. To review, an indication that there may be a problem with boundaries is the inability to say, "No," and as a result over commitment of your own time. Remember that we discussed in order to say, "Yes," to something you are effectively saying, "No," to something else—whether you intend to say, "No," to the other thing or not. The problem with saying, "Yes," all the time is that you end up committing to things you don't want to for others instead of reserving some time for yourself which leaves you feeling constantly mentally, emotionally and physically depleted.

If you answered, "True," to number two, you are not alone. Let's shift the mindset around telling people, "No," so you can feel more comfortable and confident saying, "No," to a request from another person. One perspective to take around the word "no" is that you are not saying, "No," to the *person*, you are saying, "No," to the *task* they are asking you to do. Being able to separate the person making the request from the task they are asking you to complete helps to remove the emotional connection you may have with that person. Another way to effectively say, "No," is by saying, "Yes, and…" Here is an example of how to use "Yes, and…"

Justin comes up to me and says, "Hey, it would be really great if we could take half a day on Friday afternoon and get out of the office to strategize about next quarter's company goals."

In my head I have a full plate, several projects I am working on—some for myself and some for the business and the thought of stepping away last minute for half a day to get into strategic mode seems impossible unless I can push back some project deadlines or delegate some tasks to someone else.

So, rather than just flat out saying, "No, I don't have time for that," effectively crushing his enthusiasm in the moment, I can respond with one of a couple options:

"Yes, I'd love to spend a couple hours strategizing with you and in order to do that, I would need to push back my commitment of having the new budget spreadsheet that you wanted implemented this week to next week." This puts the decision back in his court—is it worth it to him to push back that deadline in order to be able to meet with me this week?

Or...

"Yes, I'd love to spend a couple hours strategizing with you and in order to do that, I need to get a couple of these tasks on my list delegated out to someone else. Can you help with getting some of this off my plate?" Again, puts the ball back in his court. If he wants to strategize, he needs to help me out a little first.

Another tactic I have used before is honesty and open dialog about what I am being asked to do. For example, I was recently asked to volunteer for a board of directors' seat. In that moment, my ego would have totally said, "Yes," because how cool is it that someone thought highly enough of me to ask me to be on their board. But I paused for a moment and said, "I would love to commit to this position, but can I have a day or two to make sure I have enough time and space to be committed? I don't want to stretch myself too thin and not be able to meet the needs of the position."

The person that asked me was so appreciative of my honesty and the fact that I was giving the decision some thought that she would have been happy regardless of my answer. If I said, "Yes," then she would know that I considered it long enough to know that I could be totally committed to the task. If I said, "No," then she would have appreciated the fact that I recognized beforehand that I wouldn't be able to give the board the time and attention it deserved. Either way, all would have been content and no feelings would have been hurt.

3. I employ friends—hey, they need a job and I need an employee…sounds like a win/win! Besides, I trust my friend better than a stranger anyway.

This is common and can be interpreted in two ways. One way is when you employ people who were friends before they were employees and the other way is that you become friends with the people who were employees first. Either of these scenarios can be wonderful relationships as long as healthy boundaries exist. Equally, either of these scenarios can be toxic to the business and the relationship if boundaries are not in place.

A great example of the lack of boundaries (because unfortunately those stories are more common than the other way around) happened very recently with a new business owner. He and his wife had just acquired an existing plumbing company, and this was their first business. They both very much wanted the acceptance and support of the employees of the company and in an attempt to do that, they hosted regular cookouts and impromptu parties at their house. They had a lot in common with their employees and quickly became friends outside of work, regularly going out to eat and hanging out at each other's houses.

Justin and I both warned these new business owners to be very careful—they were playing in the muddy water of friends vs employees, and the employees might have a hard time separating the relationship between friend and employee. Both of the business owners shrugged off our warnings, convincing themselves that the employees knew the difference between them as friends and them as the owners of the company where they were employed.

As a coach, there are times you push an issue, and there are times you step back and watch it unfold. This was one of those lessons we felt had to be learned from their personal experience; they weren't ready to accept our warnings.

A few months as business owners, the wife was at the grocery store doing her weekly shopping. She ran into a friend that she knew through the community. They had met a few years prior when their daughters were on the same cheerleading squad. The two of them were chatting for a few minutes in the bread isle when her friend shared an experience she had with one of the technicians from their new company. The friend explained that she was running in her neighborhood and one of the company's trucks sped by, entirely too fast, and pulled into the driveway a few houses away from where she was running. As she was coming up to the house, she saw the technician was outside so she stopped and asked that he slow down because there were kids in the neighborhood, and it would be horrific if there was an accident. He blew her off, told her something about it being a long day and he had an appointment to get to with his wife. He didn't apologize, admit he was going too fast or promise to slow down in the future.

As she walked off, she said, "Well, the owners probably wouldn't appreciate you running over a kid as you race through the neighborhood."

To which he responded, "Yeah, well, I am friends with the owners, so it's all good."

The new business owner stood there in the grocery store listening to this story and was mortified, shocked, and disappointed all at the same time. She thanked her friend for sharing that experience and quickly wrapped up the conversation, so she could get out of there.

That technician was one of the employees who attended the regular and frequent cookouts they hosted, and it was clear that he could not see the boundary between being a friend and being an employee. He thought he could get special treatment or more lenient rules because he was now friends with the owners. The technician quickly learned that small town talks, and the business owners learned an invaluable lesson about boundaries. The unfortunate part about this story is that the new business owners had unintentionally created this problem, and it would take several months to get that employee culture to shift.

Let's combine questions 4, 5, and 6 and sum it up with "Hiring friends and family and treating them differently than other employees."

While this particular topic doesn't always involve your life and business partner directly, it can often cause unneeded stress on your marriage when there are unhealthy boundaries between friends and family that are employees. If you are a person who struggles with boundaries, perhaps you should steer clear of friends and family employment altogether.

Even though we see the balance more often than not fail, every now and then we are rewarded as coaches to hear about examples where the boundaries are clear and both the personal and professional relationship between the business owner and the friend/family member/employee grow and develop right along with the business.

One example of this was with a company that I coached with in Oregon. An exercise that I have my clients do early in the coaching relationship is create their Organizational Chart. If they are a company that has never had a chart of this sort in place, it's helpful for them to see the hierarchy of their business, and it's also helpful for the employees to have a visual reference to their *place on the team*. A completed and current Organizational Chart also helps me as a coach have a clear picture of who my clients are talking about when we are discussing systems creation and problem solving within their company.

This Oregon-based company completed their Organizational Chart with the position title and the first name of the employee listed under each title. We pulled out and referenced this chart often during our calls and never once did I get any indication that the people whose names were listed under each title were anything other than your standard employer/employee relationship.

One day during one of our calls, the business owner shared with me that the Office Manager was his wife's cousin, the accounting person was his daughter and one of the department managers was his daughter's boyfriend. I was blown away. Never once during our calls did he come to the conversation with an issue around drama among the relationships. Everyone was happy, everyone got along, and everyone had a very clear understanding of their place on the team and the boundaries not only surrounding their particular position on the team but also the boundaries between the personal and professional relationship. I believe he was able to keep this harmony because he's a very say-it-like-it-is kind of guy. There's no beating around the bush or vague terms coming out of his mouth. I think his very open style of communication actually helped set the clear boundaries needed to facilitate a cohesive family work environment.

Of course, the other aspect to be aware of when working with family members is how you treat them. Beware of falling into the trap of leniency toward family members. If you allow employed family members to get away with negative behavior, you are setting yourself up for animosity problems among all the employees on your team. Likewise, if you are harder on your employed family members than you are on your other employees, you could be creating an environment of resentment.

7. **I don't have a clear definition between home life and business life; I often work on business tasks at home and deal with home life issues at the office.**

This particular one was a source of conflict between Justin and me for the first several years that we owned a business. Since Justin is the visionary between us, he always has thoughts and ideas running through his head and for many years there was no filter between the thoughts that popped into his head and what or more specifically...when he shared them. On the contrary, I am the kind of person that needs a warmup period before I have to be social in the morning and in the evenings after a long day, I need some time to shut off my brain. I can usually accomplish this by doing easy tasks like housework or by simply staring through the TV during the nighttime news cast.

Justin, on the other hand, is fired up and ready to go from the second his feet hit the ground when he jumps (quite literally) out of bed to the moment he lays his head down for the night. He requires less sleep and overall less downtime than I do and because of this, he always wants to talk business. It wasn't until our business coach talked about boundaries with us that he finally started to see that I needed that separation. I needed to be able to draw a line between work and home. When I was at home and doing things around the house and with the kids, I wasn't in the mindset to talk about business and really what I needed was his presence and participation in the other half of our life that existed outside of the business. Through the facilitation of our coach, I was finally able to articulate what I needed which was for Justin to hit the pause button on working between the hours of 5-8pm and be fully present with us at the house. Prior to that facilitation, the constant barrage of business talk after my brain needed to shut down led to feelings of frustration and overwhelm on my part.

Admittedly, Justin develops tunnel vision when he's working on a new project. He's excited about it, and he begins to get up earlier and work longer hours on the new thing. The new thing begins to dominate all conversations during the day, which is fine, but in the evenings during family time, too. It has taken a long time, but we are both emotionally mature enough to see the tunnel vision coming and call it out without causing a fight or hurt feelings.

8. **My business almost always interferes with my family activities. I miss many of my kids' extra-curricular activities, and I couldn't tell you the last time I had a date night with my spouse.**

This one strikes a chord with me and brings up memories of many family activities that Justin missed because he was working, or he was present but was off in a corner with the phone glued to the side of his head. Time after time I would attend family functions with the kids, and Justin would have an excuse as to why he couldn't attend. I always hated having to explain to other family members why he wasn't there...again. It was difficult to explain his absence in a way that didn't make them feel unimportant to him. To them and me, he was setting the priority of the business higher than that of the family.

We talked in Chapter 2 about vision, and one of the exercises we did earlier in our business coaching experience was to write our eulogy. When Justin wrote his own eulogy, there was finally a much-needed shift in his mindset, and he was easily able to re-organize his priorities. He made the connection that he was working so hard for his family, and it effectively took him away from the very people he was working so hard to support.

9.   When my spouse and I do go on a date, all we have to talk about is the business. If we vow not to talk about the business, then we sit in awkward silence listening to each other chew.

I am not going to lie. I chuckled after writing this question; how true is this?! You finally decide to go on a date with your spouse, and you swear to each other that you will spend the entire meal talking about anything but the business. And then among the buzz of the restaurant, you sit for the next hour in complete silence! For those that have children, the same can apply; vow to talk about anything but the children and again nothing but crickets.

How clearly is this scenario a testament to boundaries? If you struggle to find things to talk about with your spouse that are outside of the business, then clearly your business infiltrates every aspect of your life and some boundaries need to be set up to contain its reach to within a reasonable portion of your life.

10.   I don't have hobbies outside of my business. Hobbies?! Yeah, right—who has time for those??!!

This question is more about having the free time and mental capacity to spend on a hobby not necessarily the hobby itself. Spending that time away from the business, mentally and physically, gives you the space to allow great things and great ideas to flow. We get so jammed up in the day to day fires that we leave no room for mental breaks. I have been in situations where I have been so overwhelmed with tasks that the thought of spending a little time working on a hobby was laughable and even added to the sense of overwhelm.

The metaphor I have used over time to explain this overwhelm is to picture a free-flowing river. Overwhelm acts as a dam in the river, holding back the water, preventing free flow. As the dam gets larger, the river's flow slows and slows until eventually it stops flowing at all. Then the non-flowing water becomes stagnant and so do new ideas and the ability to efficiently and effectively problem solve.

Free time can begin to punch holes in the dam. Free time gives space, even if it's just a little space, to allow the river to begin to flow again. With the movement of the water, the release of the overwhelm begins as does the flow of ideas from your brain.

We have spent quite a bit of time in this chapter showing you how to identify when there are missing or inappropriate boundaries, but we haven't spent much time on how to set up healthy boundaries once you've identified the breach. Here are a few tips on setting up healthy boundaries.

Know your limits. Think about what you can accept in physical, emotional, mental and spiritual limits. What makes you feel uncomfortable or stressed? Knowing what we can accept and what causes stress allows us to begin to identify our own limits. Everyone is different and we all draw our line in the sand at different levels. What's your line in the sand?

Pay attention to your feelings and be self-aware. Notice when you start to feel discomfort and/or resentment with a situation or relationship because that is a good sign you are nearing your boundary. Boundaries can be thought of like guard rails on the side of the road. The guard rails are there to keep you from severe danger like driving off a cliff but even if you brush up against the guardrail without ever crossing the line, there will be consequences in the form of body damage. Discomfort and resentment caught early can be easily repaired like scratched paint. Pay attention to those feelings as soon as they present themselves, so you don't find yourself over the edge of the cliff.

Communicate clearly and enforce the boundaries you have set. Not only do you need to be clear on your boundaries, you have to stick to them! Enforcing boundaries can feel emotionally difficult at the time but in the long run, it benefits both sides of the relationship. I will offer up a word of caution—too strict of boundaries and you could find yourself in isolation so be careful, but don't be afraid to stick up for yourself and your core values.

Setting and sticking to your boundaries can bring up a lot of emotions like fear, guilt or self-doubt. How will my loved ones react when I enforce my boundaries? Will they feel hurt or disappointment? Release those feelings of guilt and fear; set your boundaries and stand by them. Don't let the potential reaction of an employee, friend or family member dictate your personal limits. That's for you to decide, not them.

Consider how your family role during childhood may positively or negatively affect your ability to set and maintain boundaries. Perhaps you took on the role of caretaker early on and now in an adult setting, a self-care boundary feels selfish. Or maybe as a child you didn't want to disappoint your parents and saying, "No," meant you were being defiant therefore making it nearly impossible to say, "No," as an adult. When you begin to notice the warning signs of getting too close to your line in the sand, think about what underlying beliefs are at play and whether it is a childhood belief that is time to outgrow.

Make self-care a priority. I spent some time working in the financial department of a non-profit hospice. The amount of love and grief that cycled through that place was enough to take the average person down within days. The hospice administrator at the time, who was a fabulous leader, mentor and dare I say, family member of mine (gasp!), drilled the importance of self-care into the hospice staff. She recognized that hospice was extremely emotionally draining work, and she also knew that if the staff didn't make the time to take care of themselves, they would have no fuel in the tank to care for the hospice patients and their families. It was from her that I learned about the importance of self-care. We are all human. We are not invincible, and we must take the time to take care of ourselves so we can continue to serve our purpose. Remember, on the airplane you place your oxygen mask on first before helping others.

Setting and sticking to boundaries, without a doubt, is the most difficult skill to master especially when you are married to your business partner or you employ friends or family. However, doing so makes finding the balance between business and life possible. You'll never find true balance without boundaries.

CHAPTER 8

Strong Body, Strong Mind

"Balance myself first so I can then support the rest."
—Kristen Deese, personal mission statement

KRISTEN

I realize this book focuses on running a business when your business partner is your spouse, and a lot of what we discuss within these chapters are outwardly focused. This chapter, however, is going to be inwardly focused. Health, balance and happiness is so crucial to the success of your business and your marriage that we are dedicating an entire chapter to the topic.

Several years ago, at the beginning of our coaching journey we did an exercise around the creation of our personal mission statement or mantra. It was a multi-step process that included making a list of all our core values and whittling them down to three or four that really resonated deep in our souls. Justin and I did the exercises separately, and we each came up with our own personal mission statements.

This work led me to my personal mission statement that, to this day, still resonates deep in my soul. It keeps me grounded and reminds me that if I am to support my family and those that mean the most to me, I first must take care of myself. The foundation of the house needs to be solid, or the house will crack, weaken and eventually crumble.

There is a reason why all the airlines instruct their passengers to place the oxygen masks on themselves before helping others during an emergency. It's not selfish; it's necessary. You must take care of yourself, so you can be there for your husband, wife, kids, and business.

Owning a business can be stressful. Having your spouse as your business partner has the potential of being even more stressful than the former alone. There are countless studies and articles about the effects of chronic stress on the body.

Research agrees on a couple of side effects from stress including:

1. Increased heart rate and blood pressure which over time could lead to hypertension, heart attack and stroke.
2. Muscle tension, weight gain, headaches, loss of sleep, adrenal fatigue.
3. Digestive and gastrointestinal issues including heartburn, constipation and leaky gut.

The stress response, also known as the fight, flight or freeze response to a life-threatening situation is a hardwired response designed to keep us alive and has done a very good job at that through the thousands of years humans have been in existence. What I did not realize, but learned while doing research on how stress effects the body, was that the brain and central nervous system cannot tell the difference between life threatening being-chased-by-a-bear stress and stress caused by being stuck in a traffic jam or worrying about money or relationships.

Basically, to the brain, central nervous system and body, stress is stress - plain and simple. And, long periods of stress, even low-level stress places a constant strain on the body causing symptoms listed above plus a whole host of additional systems like depression, fatigue, endocrine disruption and hormone imbalances.

One aspect of being a successful business owner is effectively managing stress—because let's be real here, there is no such thing as a non-stress business. Managing your stress and making time for selfcare can go a long way to curb the side effects associated with stress. Following a well-balanced diet and exercise plan is also crucial for managing stress and keeping the body and mind healthy. As Buddha has so wisely said, "To keep the body in good health is a duty; otherwise, we shall not be able to keep our mind sharp and clear."

Justin has spent most of adulthood on the rollercoaster of healthy living. Over the years he has made dramatic swings from unhealthy stall patterns—consuming a bit too many French fries and hops - to healthy upswings like regular exercise with lots of veggies and lean protein - and he can absolutely make a connection between the difference in mental capacity from one side to the other. His unhealthy downswings most directly correlate with his level of stress and lack of focus and direction. When stress levels are up, especially when he's busy with a lot of irons in the fire, the healthy eating and exercise falls off the tracks. The other tasks at hand take priority over his health, and the green juices and daily 3 mile runs fall by the wayside. Then when life is easier and the pace has slowed down, the green juices and regular exercise routines resume.

Unfortunately, it's like a catch twenty-two. Really what his body needs during times of increased stress is the nutrition and exercise to keep pushing forward - and he knows this - but "knowing" and "doing" are two different beasts. I am sure you can relate, right?

I too have experienced the side effects of a long-term high stress lifestyle. A couple years ago we decided to move our family from Florida to Phoenix. We had the relocation all planned out. Everyone was on board and everyone was excited—including me. I was positively anticipating the move so much that I had even started noticing and getting irritated by all the things I disliked about where we lived in Florida. I was ready to go somewhere—anywhere—else.

The first three months after we moved to Arizona was crammed full of all the tasks associated with moving a family of four (and a dog) across the country. Getting the kids enrolled and settled in school, establishing a new pediatrician, orthodontist, vet, and new after school activities and sports teams. There was also learning my way around a new city, finding the best grocery stores, and the super important stuff like finding a new hair and nail salon. (Hey, we all have our own priorities!) On top of all that, we still had our businesses back east that needed some attention—not a lot thankfully, but regardless it was another aspect in which to spread myself even thinner. It was a lot and I was too busy to pay any attention to myself.

Once the initial ruckus of getting settled in a new state calmed down, I found myself physically, emotionally and mentally exhausted. I had no energy, I was unable to focus or concentrate, I was unorganized—to put it simply, I just was not myself. I wasn't exercising, I was making poor food choices and had discovered a taste for good craft beer. I had spent so much time and effort making sure the kids were finding their place and making friends that I didn't have the time or energy to do the same for myself. I did manage to volunteer a couple times in an attempt to find a new social circle but, admittedly, they were half-assed attempts. I definitely missed the comfortable predictability of our life in Florida.

By month five of our cross-country move, I had begun to feel the physical effects of the stress I hadn't been managing. My digestive system went haywire. Anytime I ate anything I immediately experienced intense stomach pain and nausea—so much so that it made me not want to eat. I spent hours searching my symptoms online, scouring websites looking for the magic that would fix me. I finally self-diagnosed gall stones and headed to a doctor for a second opinion. I sat in this doctor's office in tears and very hungry because by this point being hungry was better than the pain caused by eating.

After an ultrasound of my gallbladder came back clean, I was diagnosed with heartburn and sent home with a prescription for an antacid and an order to call him in six to eight weeks if I wasn't better. I was even more disheartened with the outcome of seeing a doctor...I know my body better than that. I know what heartburn feels like, and this was absolutely NOT heartburn. I left his office that day feeling unheard and not important enough to get more than seven minutes of his attention regarding an issue that, to me, was vitally important. (Maybe he should read Chapter 5 and learn better communication skills.)

By this time, I was five weeks into this mysterious digestive malfunction. I had whittled my diet down to a handful of things that I could consume without too much discomfort— with no help from the aforementioned doctor, I might add. And in addition to this, I was also trying to keep my responsibility plates spinning among three businesses and two kids through crazy fatigue and brain fog.

I had a last-minute trip planned back to Florida for a few days coming up, and Justin had decided we all needed a little break. So, the three of them scrambled to get a flight and all four of us ended flying back for a visit.

Our visit back to Florida was in late spring, a great time of year to be there, and we spent five days enjoying the beach and visiting with friends and family. By day four of our five-day trip, it became clear to Justin and me that this was where we needed to be. We belonged here. The kids belonged here. This was home.

As soon as the decision was made to come back to Florida, my digestive system began to heal. All this time I had been homesick, literally physically ill from the stress of what we had done. From that point on, not once was I in pain or ill from eating, and I was able to incorporate most foods back into my diet. I was not 100 percent back to my old self, but I was at least seeing improvement.

That's not to say that no good things came from moving to Arizona; after all, everything happens for a reason. Much like all of our other adventures as a family, we met some wonderful people, experienced cool new things, and enjoyed the incredible hiking.

A few months after we returned home, I was still out of balance emotionally. I was enjoying a significant reduction in stress; however, something still wasn't quite right. I was still experiencing fatigue, lack of focus and moodiness, but I was not about to see a traditional doctor because I knew they would half listen for five minutes and send me off with a prescription for an anti-depressant. That's not what I wanted—I wanted to fix the underlying problem, not put a bandaid over the symptoms.

I again consulted the world wide web—because everything you read on the internet is true, right? This time I came across a term that was new to me called bio-hacking. Even though the term was new to me, the concept was familiar. Essentially, bio-hacking is the idea that every human body functions better from slightly different ingredients, so you must experiment with different bio-hacks in order to find the right combination for your body to function at its personal best. Bio-hacking looks at not only what you eat, but also when you eat, when and how you exercise, what chemicals you are coming in contact within your environment and how your thoughts impact your overall health and wellbeing.

Through my research on bio-hacking, I learned the true definition of a functional doctor. I knew there were doctors out there that looked at the body holistically, but I didn't know what they were called and therefore didn't know how to find them. Turns out what I was looking for was a functional doctor, and they differ from traditional doctors in that they search for the underlying causes of any symptoms you are having in order to dial into your very best overall health.

One of the first things my new doctor did was order a few benchmarking tests. He ordered a comprehensive blood draw to evaluate the macro and micronutrients, cholesterol, hormone levels, etc. He also ordered a test to measure the amount of cortisol in my system during different times of the day. (Remember, cortisol is the hormone produced by the body when you are stressed.)

Once the results came back, we sat down and went over them in great detail. The levels of nearly everything he checked came back in the range of normal. Meaning, had a traditional doctor ordered the same blood test, they would have said I was perfectly fine. But what is the definition of "normal?" And just because I fall in the American Medical Association's definition of normal doesn't mean it's normal for me. He said, "We don't want normal. We want optimal for you." It was such a relief to be working with a doctor that continued to find answers beyond the "normal" results.

I finally felt heard, understood and not alone in my quest to regain the balance I had been searching for so long. He identified a few areas that we needed to focus on to achieve "optimal," starting with some food eliminations and tweaking my hormone levels. Within a few short weeks I was finally coming out of my funk. My mind was clear, my energy level was up, and I was feeling so much better.

Moral of my story? If you don't pay attention to your body, it will eventually get your attention, and probably in an undesirable way.

If you did an internet search on tips for managing stress, you'd see pages upon pages of results. I'll spare you the hours of reading those articles and list out a few of my favorite stress management techniques and healthy habits worth adopting. I like all of these because they are easy and not very time con-suming, so some or all of them can be seamlessly adopted by even the busiest bees.

- Meditation/deep breathing—Justin used to think meditation was only for those adorned in tie-dye and smelling of patchouli, but then he started to notice that many of his highly successful colleagues were meditating so he gave it a try and loved it. Meditation has been practiced for thousands of years. It's a practice of present moment awareness that connects us to our deepest selves. In just a few deep breaths, we can convince our central nervous system that we are not in a life or death situation and therefore out of the stress response. The deep breaths lower our heart rate and blood pressure allowing the body and mind to calm down, relax and just be. There are many apps available to take you through guided meditation, I encourage you to give it a try. If you already meditate, kick it up a notch by adding visualization to your practice.
- Gratitude exercises—Every single day complete this sentence: Today I am grateful (for/that) ___ _____ because _____. Don't just think of some-thing you are grateful for, think about why you are grateful for it, too. Be consciously grateful for the little things just as much as the big things. And for those that are more advanced in the exercise of gratitude, find the why under the why. For exam-ple: "Today I am grateful that it's Friday because it's the end of a long week. Why? Because that means

I can spend the weekend hanging out with Justin and the kids and that's one of my favorite things to do." Bonus tip: tap into your inner rebellion and write it somewhere fun like your bathroom mirror or even better your car window so you are reminded of your gratitude throughout the day.

- Journaling—This is a great way to express thoughts that might otherwise never see the light of day. It can be permission to say anything you want without repercussion. Journaling doesn't have to take on a certain form. It can be cartoons, doodles, bullet points, incomplete sentences, bad grammar and mis-spellings. Who cares if it's imperfect and the thoughts are unorganized? No one sees it but you, and it's a fabulous way to release thoughts that rattle around in the brain.

- One hour per week on your hobby—that's not too much to ask nor is it selfish, just one hour out of 168 hours each week to spend time on your hobby. Is it golf? Paddle boarding? Hiking? Scrapbooking? Dancing? Singing? Doesn't matter what it is, just do it.

- Good night's sleep—Eight hours is a must. I call malarkey on those that insist they function perfectly fine on four to five hours of sleep. If you wish you could sleep for eight hours but can't, then find out what keeps you from a good night's rest. Get to the bottom of it and solve it so you can sleep. Food for thought: eating healthy and exercising promotes sleep, and alcohol inhibits sleep. A good relationship with a functional doctor can help solve your lack of sleep issues as well.

- Healthy food choices—The right food is fuel, the wrong food sucks the life right out of you, and we are all fueled by different things. Remember a few pages back when I talked about bio-hacking? Food is a key component for hacking into your body's ideal formula and reach peak performance.

- Eat slower—It takes 20 minutes for the brain to register that the stomach is full. This is the prime culprit that leads to overeating. We are in a rush at lunch and a few minutes after we have crammed the last bite down our throat, we are overcome with the all too familiar realization that we've eaten too much. That's because we were full ten bites ago, but since it takes 20 minutes for our brain to register that signal from our stomach, and we are scarfing down lunch in five minutes flat, we are now leaning back in our chair uncomfortably wishing there was some elastic in our waistbands. Slow down, take one bite at a time and try to avoid working through lunch. When you are stressed and eating fast, your body doesn't allocate the right amount of energy to digestion. This means you aren't pulling the maximum amount of nutrition from each bite, and your meal just sits there in your stomach like a rock. Allow your body to focus on digestion so it can pull the nutrients from the food you are eating to keep you going strong until the next meal.

- Daily exercise or movement of some sort—Move in some way, shape or form every day and kick it up from moderate to intense exercise at least three times each week. Go to the gym, hire a personal trainer, attend a regular fitness class—anything that gets your heart rate up and works your muscles. The endorphins produced from exercise are like a little army of stress busters and mood boosters.

- Keep an even keel—Avoid blood sugar roller coasters and eliminate the mid-day slump by not skipping meals or not eating heaving lunches. Skipping breakfast and eating a lunch full of simple carbs (like a hamburger and super-sized French fries) is the perfect combination for the mid-day slump. Stay energized the entire day by eating a healthy breakfast and a lunch that contains leafy greens and lean protein.

- Date night once or twice per month is a great activity to stay connected and provide simultaneous selfcare. It's very easy to lose the intimate connection with your spouse when you work and live with them. It's also easy to be too busy or too tired to spend quality time with your spouse—I am sure you've heard it before, but schedule date nights and enjoy some time reconnecting as husband and wife, not just business partners.

- Reading for pleasure is a popular form of selfcare. Sometimes it's fun to lose yourself in a romantic or mystery novel. It can be a nice brain break from the ever-popular business and self-help books.

- Hire a health coach—we all need a certain level of accountability in our lives and if incorporating a healthy food and exercise routine into your lifestyle poses as a challenge, a health coach could be the solution. Health coaches are specifically trained in habit change and can provide tons of tips and tricks on how to make a healthy transition from treating your body like a frat house to treating it like a temple.

- Encourage healthy activities in the workplace— Every year we pay for our employees to enter a 5k. It benefits a good local cause, and it promotes a healthy lifestyle. One client I coached purchases gym memberships as part of the business's benefit package but in order to keep the membership, they must attend the gym at least 4x per month. As a positive, unintended consequence, he found his employees were bonding at the gym before work, holding each other accountable and contributing to a positive company culture.

Take some time to communicate with your spouse what your selfcare activities are and mark them on your calendar. Communicating with your spouse about your selfcare is another opportunity for them to learn the *why* behind the things you do—and vice versa. If your form of selfcare is uncustomary or not obvious to your spouse, then talking about it makes them more aware. One of my forms of selfcare is shopping. Sometimes I like to wonder through the racks of clothes at the store. Most of the time I don't buy anything, but I enjoy the solitude and brain break. Your spouse is far more likely to support and encourage your selfcare activities when that door of communication is open…and you will be more understanding of your spouse.

We've created a quiz so you can rate yourself on your current level of health and balance. Read each question and rate them on a number scale between 1 and 10, where "1" means *never* and "10" means *always.* Your goal should be a "10" for every single question and if it's not a "10," take some time to consider what would need to happen in your life to make it so.

I wake up every day energized and ready to attack the day with enthusiasm.

Score_____

I don't rely on coffee to "wake up" in the morning or stay awake in the afternoon.

Score_____

I feel focused and clear minded at least 90% of the time.

Score_____

I eat at least four servings of both colorful, organic fruit and veggies each day.

Score_____

I do not skip meals, and my food consumption is on a regular schedule.

Score_____

I drink at least half my body weight in ounces of water each day.

Score_____

I keep my alcohol consumption to no more than three drinks per week.

Score_____

I get at least eight hours of restful sleep each night.

Score_____

I make sure to incorporate selfcare into my daily routine.

Score_____

I incorporate exercise of some sort into my weekly routine.

Score_____

Total score _____

So, how did you do? Are there some areas in your health that need some attention? Sit down with your spouse, review each other's answers and come up with some ideas and a plan for each of you to achieve less stress and more balance in your lives.

If you can get to a point where you are consistently answering "9" or better for every single question, you will find reflections of the positive side effects of those high scores in all aspects of your life—your marriage, your business and your relationships.

CHAPTER 9

Reaping the Benefits

"The best feeling in the world is seeing the benefits and rewards of hard work." —Kevin Hart

This book dug into many of the hardships that we have faced over the years, and we felt as though if we struggled in these areas, there was a good chance other couples who are navigating the challenging terrain of running their own businesses together are struggling as well. After we started coaching, it became clear there were many commonalities we saw between what we experienced and what our clients were experiencing. It has become our mission to seek out and help those that are in the shoes we were in, so they can thoroughly enjoy what they have painstakingly created—rather than resent it.

What we'd like to do now is share a story about how our life has changed by tackling struggles and hardships in the manner described in the previous chapters. We spent a great deal of time over the last several years changing and shaping the way our company runs. Our goal was for it to serve us, not us to serve it. We have done so successfully. As a result, we were able to take a three month road trip across the US in our RV—something we never would have been able to do before we implemented the items we discussed throughout this book—and completely change the way we ran our business.

We participated in our epic cross-country adventure with a couple hundred Facebook followers, and we'd like to share some of what we posted during our trip with you.

Day 0, the day after Christmas: We spent ALL day yesterday packing the RV and preparing the house for departure. Not only did we have to pack, but we needed to put away all the Christmas decorations, too. After all, we won't return for a while and we don't want to be *those neighbors* that have Christmas lights up until spring.

I've been asked a couple times how did I pack for 60 days on the road? To that I say—I have no clue! But those of you who know me well can probably guess I started with a little research to decide what to bring. After looking up weather trends in the areas we will be spending most of our time, I came to the conclusion that our everyday clothes need to keep us comfortable in the 55-75-degree range. That's not bad, I can do that. So, everyone has 7-10 days of clothes for that temperature. We don't have a washer/dryer on board so laundry will be done in laundromats, and I don't want to be there more than once a week, hence the decision to stock 7-10 days. Tucked away in some of the various not-so-easy to get to storage compartments I have stashed swimsuits and a little bit of cold weather gear just in case we find ourselves swimming or sledding.

We have bikes hanging on the back of the rig and the kids' scooters tucked away underneath along with some fun outdoor games and activities for evenings at the campgrounds.

Inside we have games, games and more games! We have internet, but it's not going to be as fast as it is at home so while streaming TV is possible, it's not likely going to be at the top of the list of things to pass the time. I consider us a pretty close family, but I am looking forward to this trip bringing us even closer and cutting down on the TV time will help with that ☺

I have most of the basic food prep gadgets on board needed to make just about anything we would eat at home. The main difference is the lack of counter space and refrigerator space. Ideally, we'll stock up on fresh fruits, veggies and meats every three days or so. And of course, we have the Ninja, because like a visa card, we can't leave home without it!

Fourteen hours of packing and prepping, we should have everything we need for three months on the road.

Even though we will be seeing and doing all kinds of cool and crazy things, we will still miss our friends and family! We hope by posting our trip across the county we can stay connected to everyone we love and meet some new friends along the way. Follow us on this page and invite your friends to follow us too, and we'll see you in a couple months!

Day 1: Today begins our adventure across the country! We all are experiencing so many emotions on this day. The kids are excited about the cool things we will be doing and seeing on the road but at the same time a little sad they won't be seeing their friends for several weeks. Justin and I are super excited too, and a little nervous. Even though we have spent the last couple of weeks planning, there are still quite a bit of unknowns.

Nonetheless, we shoved off at 8:30 am and drove a total of 394 miles. It took a little longer than expected; the roads in Mississippi are horrible which kinda slowed us down! We stopped for a couple hours in Jackson, MS to have a break. There we toured the Mississippi Museum of Natural Science. That was pretty cool; more than half of Mississippi used to be under water!

Tonight, we boon dock in West Monroe, LA. This is home to Duck Dynasty and in the morning, we'll go duck hunting (not real ducks, just the Robertson's).

We managed to eat three round meals on the RV today, and I used my convection/microwave for the first time tonight. Cooked up some okra that we got at a roadside stand in the middle of nowhere Mississippi. Now, everyone is taking some time (yes, even the kids) to journal about their day—a ritual I hope we can keep up throughout this trip.

Day 3: Wondering why we named this blog "Coaching from a Coach?" This is a working trip, not all museums and adventures, although one could argue that when you are doing what you love then, every day feels like a vacation. Justin and I are both coaches. Yesterday was a great example of the definition of our blog's name.

We were able to spend a couple hours with KGS Demolition Attachment Services. They are a young company with a bright future and ready to take hold of the reigns rather than having their business gallop off with them barely hanging on. (By the way, we are in Texas. ;) Steering a company in the direction you want to go can be much easier said than done though. Especially if you aren't sure which direction you want your business to go. As we sat and talked with them yesterday, there was so much Justin and I both could resonate with. They are also a married couple trying to make their business and marriage work together. There are some days when it works beautifully, and there are some days when it just doesn't. Justin and I have been there. We have been doing the business ownership and marriage thing for many years and could relate and empathize with every area of joy and frustration this young couple expressed yesterday.

Justin and I hired a business coach a couple years ago, and that one decision changed the course of not only our business but our lives. And to be able to now work with companies and help them get on track the way our coach was able to do with us is such a wonderful feeling.

Many of the stops we have planned along our trip across the county are decided based on client locations, and we are so excited to make an impact on these businesses—and who knows? Maybe we'll be able to help others change their trajectory just like our coach did with us.

Day 4: Work hard, play hard. Justin got some good coaching done in the morning while the kids and I explored the river learning how to skip rocks. Once the work was done, Justin took the kids to the shooting range next to the campground. They got to play with a bow and arrows, a BB gun and an air pistol.

Then, in the evening, the Deeses were introduced to the Fort Worth Stockyards. What a cool experience! It was our opportunity to dress up like the locals, boots included, and enjoy a good ole' rodeo. Lucky for us, it was inside so we were nice and toasty warm, too. Addy had been to a rodeo before, but she didn't remember because the last time we went she was very little. This time she couldn't take her eyes off the arena! I could see she was experiencing the little girl dreams of growing up and riding her horse complete with hat and bedazzled chaps. She was literally sitting on the edge of her seat the entire time. ;)

Loving Texas so far.

Day 16: Today marks day 3 of homeschool with FLVS. Day 1 of homeschooling was pretty stressful for me—not for the kids I don't think. We have talked to all of Zack's teachers with the exception of Spanish. That class hasn't been opened up to him yet. And we talked to Addy's teacher, too.

Addy is in 4th grade so through FLVS she only has one teacher, besides me of course. ;) We log in on Monday mornings and get the lesson plan for the week and on Friday certain assignments are submitted to her teacher for grading and the rest we put in her portfolio to show the state we are actually doing something resembling education.

Ironically, this week in school, Addy is learning about entrepreneurs. She had to think of a business, name it, figure out who her customers were going to be, how much she was going to charge them for her product and come up with the purpose of starting the business in the first place. A little back story to her business—we are currently in an RV park in Phoenix. This particular RV park has over 600 lots, so we have spent quite a bit of time walking around the neighborhood. Some of the people who live here have orange trees on their lots. Addy's business idea was to pick the oranges off the trees and sell them to people who didn't have orange trees in their yard. She learned that she would probably have to pay the orange tree owner for the oranges she picked which means she'd have to sell the oranges for a higher amount than what she paid for them. 4th grade economics—love it! By the way—she named her business "Orange you glad I sell oranges."

Day 21: 3 weeks on the road. I'm impressed. Impressed we aren't sick of each other yet. Impressed that we are managing to get on somewhat of a routine. And impressed that it doesn't feel like we have been away from home for 21 days.

During the week we work on school. Some days it takes six hours, some days it takes four, but I know the more comfortable we get with the FLVS system, the more efficient we will be with our school time and the easier it will get. (That's true for all systems I suppose.) Like Justin says, "Everything is easy once you know how to do it."

When we are not doing school stuff, we are exploring Phoenix and Scottsdale. There is so much to do and see here! We got to do plenty of hiking last week and over the weekend and yesterday we went to the aquarium.

This week we look forward to staying in a hotel for a couple days during Justin's coaching industry event. There we will get to see a few familiar faces from home and meet new people within the service industry as well.

I am enjoying the simplicities of RV life. There is just less stuff. Less stuff in the small fridge, fewer clothes to keep up with, fewer dishes and kitchen gadgets...fewer square feet to clean! It takes like 30 minutes to clean this thing top to bottom—on the inside anyway. It actually takes longer to clean the outside! Doing the laundry at the laundromat isn't bad either. I can use several machines at the same time and get everything done quickly in 2 hours. It would have taken all day to do the same at home. There is also less to do, fewer places to be. No homework, no extracurricular activities to run out the door for and more time to just hang out and relax.

Of course, it's not all roses all the time. We have some annoyances, too. One is the ridiculously short amount of time it takes for clutter to gather in the main living area. When there is clutter, it makes it feel even smaller than it actually is. The internet is slow. Slow to the point of having to take turns streaming videos (many videos with FLVS). But it works well enough for Facebook and email so that's good. The size of the bathroom and the fact there is only one is kind of a drag too. We have to plan out who takes AM and PM showers, so there is enough hot water for all and inevitably as soon as someone gets in the shower, someone else has to go to the bathroom. ☺ Looking forward to being able to hold my arms out and not touch two walls at the same time in the hotel bathroom later this week! (It's the little things!)

Sunday we will depart Arizona and head for San Diego, CA. There I will be spending three days immersed in a coaching conference and continuing education.

Day 27: Yesterday we said, "Farewell," to Phoenix. We spent an amazing couple of days connecting with fellow entrepreneurs at an annual home services business development event. I met so many awesome people, some of which we'll see again on this trip at other shows, cities and even countries! (More on that coming soon!) Justin rocked his presentation on the importance of systems within a business and now that the event is behind us, he'll be able to relax and decompress for a little while.

During the event, we parked the RV and stayed at the hotel for a few nights. Surprisingly, by the end of the stay at the hotel, I was more than ready to get back to my home away from home. Bandit, on the other hand, thoroughly enjoyed the hotel room! On the RV, he only gets to sleep with Addy because she has the bottom bunk, but at the hotel he got to sleep in the bed with both the kids and thought he was tough stuff.

We rolled out a little before lunch. The sun was out but man, was it windy! Pretty much all 380 miles contained strong gusts of cross winds—which keeps you on your toes when you are driving a giant box down the road. We went south of Phoenix and picked up I-8 all the way to San Diego. It was an unbelievable drive! It was so cool watching the landscape change. We went from the desert valley to rolling sand dunes, where the wind was literally making the ground move, and into the mountains of southern California. We went from sea level to 4100 ft and back to sea level within just a few hours.

We got into our campground a little after dark, hooked up the RV, ate and stared through the television for about an hour before succumbing to the exhaustion that had been building for the last couple days. I don't know about Justin, but I slept good for the first time in several nights and it was fabulous. *Added bonus, we didn't have to turn the heat on for the first time since we left Florida. Score!

We woke up this morning in sunny San Diego—except it isn't sunny and it's supposed to rain this afternoon and tonight. But that's ok. We'll get out and about this morning, check out the area we are staying (Mission Beach) and spend the afternoon preparing for next week. Zack gets to be homeschooled by Dad for the first three days of the week while I am at my coaching conference. I can't wait to hear how that goes. ;)

I'll leave you today with a quote from Kenny Chapman that stuck with me from the event last week: "*What you have been doing got you your current results.*" If you don't like your results, change what you are doing! Very simple, yet true and pretty powerful.

Get ready to be blasted with San Diego pics!

Day 35: We are almost halfway through our first long RV trip and we have spent the last week in San Diego. The week started out with more rain and wind than this area has received in years, but once that gross weather finally cleared, we experienced a taste of a more typical San Diego winter. Sunny and 75. That's more like it.

Justin (and the kids) made it through three days of homeschool last week while I was at my coaching conference. Our reward for working hard all week was going to the San Diego Zoo on Friday. That was quite an experience! That is a huge zoo. The most interesting thing I learned that day was that the zoo has more money in endangered plants and trees than in animals. And, they grow their own food for the animals—most of it is on the property but they also have a farm close by where they grow the rest.

After the zoo, we met Sean Roberts and his three children at Dave and Buster's. Justin and Sean were friends in high school but haven't seen each other since they graduated. It was fun to hear them catch each other up on the last 20 years.

We spent several hours on Mission Beach on Saturday and then on Sunday morning, we went to La Jolla to see animals in their natural habitats. Sea Lions! I was surprised to see that you could walk all the way down to where they were lying. It didn't seem like a very good idea to me, especially after watching a father coax his pre-school age children down to one particular sea lion that was yelling - only to have the children run away screaming and terrified. (It still amazes me that you have to pass a test to drive a car but not to have children.) We walked down on the rocks where they were, but we kept our distance. They are slow moving, but they are still wild animals. I loved how they lay together on the rocks, napping in the warm sun. Safety and warmth in numbers. ☺

After oooing and ahhhing over the sea lions for a while we went to The Cave Store right there in La Jolla and descended 143 steps into a cave that opened up into the ocean. The outline of the opening looks like the profile of a man, and the cave entrance was built in the early 1900s to allow people to see the cave without accessing it by water. During prohibition, alcohol was carried up the 143 stairs and supplied to the bars in La Jolla.

We have a couple of quiet days here in San Diego before we head to Mexico on Thursday. Yup, you read that right! Mexico! Not for vacation though. We are going in service to a school for the deaf in Ensenada called Rancho Sordo Mudo. You can check out the school website here: http://www.ranchosordomudo.org/ I am super excited for this experience and cannot wait to report it to you!

Day 37: Just a quick little update on our trip to Mexico...we have decided to cancel that leg of the trip. I don't know if the media has been showing the border protests all over the US or just here because we are so close to the border but many of the access points to Mexico are closed due to protesters upset over gas prices in Mexico. We were also a little nervous about not being able to get back into the states even though we all have passports. While I wanted to give the kids an opportunity to see history unfolding before them, I didn't want to scare them during this turbulent political and social time in our country.

So, we are safe and sound in Oceanside, CA enjoying the next ten days or so before we head a little farther north to LA.

Last day of trip 1:

75 days
9 states

5300 miles
We did it!

The last day in the RV was such a mix of emotions for all of us. We were excited to be home but oh so grateful to experience such a trip.

Now everything is put away, the RV is at the shop for some routine maintenance (to prepare for the next trip), and we are enjoying the spaciousness of our home. ☻ :)

Stay tuned for our next trip up through the eastern states in early summer!

This was the first of several long RV trips that we were able to take as a family. The people and systems that we put in place make it possible for the businesses to continue to operate successfully without us present. We still worked during our travels, our trips are not true vacation, but we used technology to our advantage and chose to work from wherever our RV would take us. Because we are making our businesses and marriage work cohesively, we are able to experience adventures that many people don't ever get to do, and we are able to show our kids things that they would normally only see pictures of on the pages of textbooks.

We thank you for taking the time to read this creation inspired by our last 20 years together, and we sincerely hope you take

KRISTEN & JUSTIN DEESE

away and implement everything we have taught you in these pages. As mentioned before, *knowing* is different than *doing*. You'll need to actually implement what you have learned for it to have a positive impact on your business and your marriage, and we have set up a couple ways to help you do just that. We look forward to connecting with you through masterminds, group coaching and social media. Check out our website at www.businessspouse.com for information on upcoming groups and events.

EPILOGUE

From the time the first word of this book was written to the time it finally was sent to print was over two years. We started off full steam and got three quarters of it knocked out within the first few months. Then we hit a stall pattern. Writing the book was placed on the back burner, and lots of other life events moved higher on the priority list.

As discouraging and downright frustrating as it was to have this project sit idle for so long, at no point during that time did I ever even desire to work on it. I got a taste of writer's block—turns out that's a real thing!

What I am learning now though…is that everything happens for a reason. Had I finished the book at the initial pace, I wouldn't have had a lot of the content for Chapter 8. Or perhaps the content of Chapter 8 was the cause of the stall. I suppose it could be looked at either way, but regardless, the extra time it took to get it all on paper provides a great benefit to you. The nearly two-year stall allowed for that much more experience to be interwoven into these chapters.

We will always be business owners of multiple businesses; there's no doubt about that. One of the things we have discovered in recent years is Justin's love of the small business growth process. It's exciting to start a new business (or acquire an existing small, struggling one) and see how quickly we can turn it around and steer it to explosive growth. Each time we grow a business, we always start with the basics—many of which are found right here in the pages you just read.

When I finally decided to pick this project back up and get it finished, I found myself re-reading the chapters over and over. I wanted to make sure they were perfect and the words expressed our intended message in a way you could truly resonate.

Something I realized towards the end was that even after all these years of being married to my business partner, we still practice what we preach. No, it's not a perfect, harmonious balance all the time, but more often than not, it's pretty great. And when our marriage or one of our businesses starts to get a little sideways, we recognize it so much faster than we used to. What do we do when we start to slide? We go back to the basics of this book.